WHEN YOU DARE TO SAY YES

When You Dare to Say Yes

A Nevada Story

JILL DERBY

UNIVERSITY OF NEVADA PRESS | *Reno & Las Vegas*

University of Nevada Press | Reno, Nevada 89557 USA
www.unpress.nevada.edu
Copyright © 2024 by University of Nevada Press
Manufactured in the United States of America

FIRST PRINTING

Cover and frontispiece photograph © David Cohen

Library of Congress Cataloging-in-Publication Data on File
ISBN: 978-1-64779-140-7 (cloth)
ISBN: 978-1-64779-141-4 (ebook)
LCCN: 2023942819

The paper used in this book meets the requirements of American National Standard for
Information Sciences—Permanence of Paper for Printed Library Materials, ANSI/NISO
Z39.48–1992 (R2002).

To my husband, Steve Talbot, whose tireless support of my activism made every step along the way possible. He has been my rock and grounding in an adventurous ride through life since we married half a century ago, and the other half responsible for our two children, Ryan and Tobyn Derby-Talbot, without whom our world would be much less complete, satisfying, and fun.

"Your playing small doesn't serve the world. . . . [A]s we let our own light shine, we unconsciously give other people permission to do the same."

—MARIANNE WILLIAMSON, *A Return to Love: Reflections on the Principles of* A Course in Miracles

Contents

Preface

"Who, me? Run for political office?"

That was how I responded to my colleagues who were leading the Nevadans for ERA (Equal Rights Amendment) campaign of 1978. "You've got to be kidding. I wouldn't know how. I'm not the seek-the-spotlight type."

And so, I tripped backward into putting my political money where my mouth was, unwittingly altering my life's course and unlocking a multitude of unforeseen opportunities. Nothing is more exciting, engaging, and meaningful than becoming politically informed and politically active. Whether a position opens on your local school board, city council, or state legislature, I urge you to seize the opportunity to take part in one of the most rewarding adventures you will ever know.

If elective office is not your thing, seek out spots on boards and commissions, and apply. If you are questioning your credentials, let me assure you that your desire to make a difference and help steer the institutions of government and society in long-lasting positive ways is all that is required when taking that first step. The rest of the know-how you will need to launch (and to win!) a political campaign is covered in how-to books or online. A Google search will lead you to information about your local planning commission, water conservancy board, homelessness task force, and library board. Whatever your passion and cause, it is my hope that sharing my story will inspire others to step out and take a stand for something *today*.

It takes commitment and energy, but subordinating your own interests to a larger cause is enlivening, energizing, and educational. You don't win an election campaign playing alone. Once you have rallied a support team and have defined your goals, the way you set out together to achieve them creates a bond and a purpose that lasts a lifetime. You enter into a fierce competition of ups and downs to achieve a critical victory, and an "all in this together" sense of camaraderie infuses the enterprise with a vibrant and fun esprit de corps.

Win or lose an election, though it may sound contradictory, there is much to be won. The ultimate goal, of course, is to win the vote count and attain the office sought, but don't discount the skills you will gain and the many doors that will open to you simply for having signed up and run in the first place. No matter the size and sphere of influence of the office you are seeking, you will personally benefit from putting yourself out there and speaking your mind—and if at first you don't succeed, you can always try again, like me and thousands of others before me.

Running for office allows you to establish a public face and to become known in your community as someone who is willing to step out from the crowd to put forward an important cause. While many find it more comfortable to remain on the sidelines when it comes to tackling complex issues and instigating change, taking a clear and vocal stand renders you more recognizable and recruitable for future opportunities and leadership roles. When openings occur in various boards, commissions, community projects, civic or school endeavors, your name is likely to come up.

Nothing is inherently wrong with people who prefer to work in the background or from the sidelines—many find their best place cheering on and supporting others, and we need those cheers. But we need our full range of human potential to tilt the course of history in a better direction. In a time not so long ago, many women were raised to think that they belonged forever on the sidelines rather than in the field of play. Those days are over. The world needs women leaders with the human sensitivities, people-focus, and social-emotional skills they bring to the table.

The world needs more enlightened men too, pursuing positions of power and influence in the public sphere. Fortunately, women have had male support over the decades—men who have seen the benefits of participating in the creation and sustainability of a more level playing field for the women in their lives. Many sons recall the hardships and disadvantages their mothers faced, and many fathers want a much fairer start and shake for their daughters.

"Am I the type to run for public office?"

If you are asking yourself this question, let me assure you, the answer is "yes." You have this book in your hands and once you are off and running, you will rise to the occasion and be the better for it, whatever the outcome. Playing big makes you bigger, so get ready to expand your horizons. What you do becomes part of who you are, and by seeking out new adventures, you become an adventurer. Trust that the challenges along the path ahead will call forth in you the skills you need to meet and overcome them.

If you fear public speaking, sign up for Toastmasters and start speaking. If you are not gifted at addressing the issues, study them. If asking for people's support gives you a case of the jitters, trust that most people are receptive and want to help, so ask for what you need. If you hear "yes," congratulations and keep moving forward; if you hear "no," don't take it personally—move on. Some doubts and fears are well-founded, but most of the negative "what if" and "not-up-to-it" scenarios we create, along with the stories we tell ourselves about our own inadequacies, are just stories we or someone else made up about us long ago.

It is time to stop listening to these worn-out, self-doubting inner narratives. Start a new chapter; bring out that new you.

None of us is stuck, and none of our realities are cast in stone. We are a work in progress; our systems (education, health care, employment, human services) are works in progress too. Our choices determine who we become individually and collectively, and the more we learn and take action, the more fun and satisfying it is to play the game of running for office, winning a coveted role or position, and making a difference. You will learn the game; if I did, you can.

Forty years ago, by simply saying "yes" in the face of daunting circumstances and the unknown, I ran my first race. A world of opportunity opened, and I began to expand my horizons in ways I hadn't foreseen.

Where to begin? Look around. What grabs your passion? In which decision-making chambers would you like your voice to be heard? Start there, and trust that the rest will unfold. Commitment, pluck, and courage all come into play once you make the choice to take politics into your own hands, but finding your place in the public arena starts with your desire to weigh in and make a difference—so, go for it!

Democracy depends on active and engaged citizens to make it work. If citizens are not involved at every level of public policy deliberations—local, state, and national—a vacuum is left for power, partisan, and monied interests to sway outcomes in their own interests. As rewards for individual striving have increasingly been emphasized, the concept of the "common good" has fallen out of use in the political lexicon. The focus on broad-based benefits for policy outcomes needs to be reinstated. Having an array of citizens involved in policy decisions is more likely to represent and serve the needs and interests of the many. Putting the emphasis back on the "we" of "we the people" is the only way to protect our democracy and ensure our democracy—our *United* States—moves forward.

Albert Einstein said, "The world is a dangerous place, not because of those who do evil, but because of those who look on and do nothing."

There are multiple opportunities and ways of affecting the system and making your voice heard. The nonpartisan, multi-issue group Nevadans for the Common Good (NCG) has acquired considerable political clout in the Nevada Legislature. Originally organized by faith communities in Las Vegas, NCG is now a network of labor, civic, educational, nonprofit, and faith-based organizations that has made strides in eliminating homelessness and hunger and in providing greater access to health care and education for those most in need. This kind of leadership training, community building, and citizen activism is what is needed to advocate for the common good and to balance the scales in this era of partisan divide, special monied interests, and corporate political dominance.

Seeking public office gives each and every one of us a chance to make a difference, and it is the course I chose. I hope my story of unexpectedly running for political office and all the opportunities to bring leadership and to influence public policy that followed offers a glimpse of a highly satisfying life pathway. Though I had little idea what saying "yes" would entail, and though I had much to learn every step of the way, at the end of the day—every day—I know I can say, "I did my part."

Acknowledgments

More than twenty years ago, my best friend since third grade, author Drusilla Campbell, urged me to write a memoir. She knew my life up close from many shared adventures and decades of letters, tapes, phone calls, and visits. "Your story is worth the printed page," she urged. My activist schedule didn't slow down until the 2020 pandemic kept me at home, on Zoom, with space to write something longer than an article or opinion piece. Along with our decades of friendship, I am eternally grateful for a seed she planted that finally sprouted. If she had lived, she would have read and cheered me on through every chapter and draft.

Writing the first draft of this book was almost easier than sorting out an order and flow to the narrative that wove a multidecade story together into a readable weave. I owe a great debt of gratitude to my writing coach and editor, Christine Fadden, whose expertise in story choreography and editing skill made it all come together in the end. Equally important was her constant encouragement and the warm friendship that developed between us. Her professional guidance and support were invaluable.

My niece, Kelly Lavino, has my love and special gratitude for all the time she spent transcribing reels of cassette tapes I used in correspondence over decades when letters were the only other option for staying in touch over distances. I began the practice of recording and sending tapes to family and friends during my years in Saudi Arabia and continued the practice during my commuting hours while in graduate school. Having many of these spoken letters in written form was an important nudge to my memory. Kelly, too, has always been a cheerleader in my corner, and her support and love have been a wind in my sails for many years.

I owe a special debt of gratitude to historian Caryll Batt Dziedziak, PhD, director of the Women's Research Institute of Nevada on the University of Nevada, Las Vegas, campus. Her 2010 dissertation, "The Gendering of Nevada Politics: The ERA Ratification campaign,

1973–1981," was invaluable to me in my efforts to recall the dates, facts, and names of that decade now fifty years past. Without her contribution to the history of Nevada's long struggle to advance the status of women, a seminal chapter in that long struggle would be largely lost to posterity. She captured it all and wrote it so well.

Warren Lerude, author, Pulitzer Prize–winning journalist, and towering figure in northern Nevada's twentieth-century history, early on encouraged me to keep writing the book I had begun. Having his affirmation was a boost in confidence that kept me returning to my desk and laptop.

Pat Hickey, former Nevada legislator, columnist for the *Reno Gazette-Journal*, and author, whom I first got to know while serving together on the Guinn Center board, was in a parallel process of writing a book. I am grateful for the advice and support he offered in the spirit of friendship and collegiality.

My gratitude goes to the staff at the University of Nevada, Reno, Special Collections Library, who were most helpful in assisting me to retrieve documents, fliers, papers, and press accounts that I had donated to the Nevada Women's History Project archives decades ago. Time frays memory, and without access to those files, some facts and names would have been lost to me.

Special thanks to Joanne Goodwin, former director of UNLV's Women's Research Institute of Nevada, for her part in the production of *Makers: Women in Nevada History* series, an interview I did in the nineties that also jogged my memory of activities decades ago.

The staff at the University of Nevada Press has been a pleasure to work with at every step. I am in special debt to Curtis B. Vickers, acquisitions editor, who gave me much-needed advice in my early interactions with the Press and was abundantly supportive. He was patient in walking me through the steps required for publication at the Press—foreign territory for me. Vickers is a fine asset to the University of Nevada Press, particularly to novice authors. Special thanks to copy editor Paul Szydelko, who was a delight to work with and whose thorough fact-checking and editing skills left me confident and relaxed as my book headed off for the printing press.

I have three very special Nevada friends who have been there for me since I first stepped out of the bleachers and onto the court of public activism: Judy Williams, Constance Alexander, and Lynne

Parish. Having close women friends is one of life's great treasures—a buffer against the "thousand natural shocks that flesh is heir to" and a safe space of warmth, support, and validation as the years roll by. I could not have done what I have done without them. We have stayed close and in common cause over the decades, and today we call our foursome "the Sirens." We meet regularly on Zoom to share life happenings, great reading, and conversations about things that matter.

My family, who holds my heart and my center of gravity, deserves the greatest appreciation of all. I owe them a world of gratitude for allowing me the space and energy to step out in the marketplace of life and seek to have an impact in causes of civic engagement and passion. My husband, Steve, who on occasion lets me know he is proud to be married to me—has been my rock and anchor since the day we married. Steve is loved by everyone. Hardly a month goes by without my being stopped in the local supermarket by someone telling me how much they love my husband. Being married to a veterinarian has extra perks, too, particularly in a house shared with dogs and cats and occasionally wounded kids. On top of that, vets are a special breed of human being. Ask any animal lover about theirs.

I drew the best card in the deck with my daughter, Tobyn, who has been unequaled company and support. I could not have wished for more over the years of activities and adventures we have shared. Whether cheering an election win or consoling after losses, she has always been there for me. Her role of being at my side began with her flying with me in the state plane to regents' meetings in Elko when she was eight, and it continued through recent years accompanying me to my board meetings in Iraqi Kurdistan. Her incomparable spirit of fun and count-on-able support are treasures that have filled my years with comfort and joy.

It is a delight to share my world of higher education with my son, Ryan, who has served in four different countries as university professor, dean, chief academic officer, and vice president. He's learned three foreign languages in the process—Japanese, Arabic, and Vietnamese. We have been good sounding boards for each other in this distinctly challenging arena of academic governance and leadership. His acquired savvy in how to work effectively with all kinds of actors in the academic environment (no small achievement) has served me well.

WHEN YOU DARE TO SAY YES

CHAPTER I

What? Me Run?

In 1977, I joined the Nevada ERA Steering Committee at the urging of friends, mainly because the organizers wanted a representative from a northern rural county, and ERA supporters were few and far between in my part of the state. Actually, as we were about to discover, there were very few of us, derisively labeled "women libbers," in all of Nevada.

We were up against the headwinds of ultraconservative voters such as those who live in Douglas County, with its then 80 percent–plus Republican majority. Statewide and nationwide, a narrative had been spun that the passage of the ERA would "interfere" with women choosing motherhood, put women in military combat roles, destroy families, and generally wreak havoc on the social fabric of America. As is often true, it is easier to make a case against something than a case for it, especially when "the something" has never been tried and there are a host of unknowns.

While contemporary generations may have read of the feminist fight of the seventies, it can be all too easy to forget how close on each generation's shoulders the succeeding generations stand. For twentysomethings, the chances are great that their grandmothers had to fight to enter certain professions such as medicine, law, journalism, or economics. Those same grandmothers never had a chance to pursue athletics beyond school sports, while today we cheer on the US women's soccer team for winning World Cups. The contrast is stark. The then-to-now scenario happened because of the "then" women who stepped out of line and called foul to the gender rules that kept them in the locker room and off the playing field. The lesson learned is that today's mavericks may be the prophets of tomorrow's mainstream.

The origins of the ERA extend back two centuries to the 1840s and the beginning of the women's suffrage movement. Although women won the right to vote in 1920 after a long and bitter eighty-year struggle, many early feminists believed that achieving the right to vote would result in full equality for women. As a result, after suffrage was achieved, many leaders of the women's movement laid down their posters and picket signs and turned to other causes protective of women. A small cadre of those leaders, however, were skeptical and stayed the course.

Alice Paul, a Quaker who was not afraid of facing jail time and conducting hunger strikes, leader of the National Woman's Party, spearheaded the drive to enshrine women's equality in the US Constitution in the form of a constitutional amendment guaranteeing women equal rights under the highest law of the land. Paul's efforts began to come to fruition in 1923, when Kansas senator Charles Curtis, a Republican, introduced the Equal Rights Amendment in the US Congress. A forty-nine-year, contentious political struggle would ensue.

In 1972, the ERA received a majority vote in the US Senate and was sent out to the fifty states for ratification. A compromise that had been hammered out in committee to achieve a majority vote in the US Senate set a restrictive and unprecedented seven-year time limit on the ratification process as the amendment moved into the jurisdiction of state legislatures.

According to the requirement for adding an amendment to the Constitution, three-fourths (or 38) of the states must ratify it once it achieves the US Senate's stamp of approval. A political fight that had been confined to the national stage for five decades was thus transferred to states and their legislatures. Within a relatively short time period, thirty states ratified the ERA. As the process moved forward, supporters, movers, and shakers focused on identifying the eight additional states mostly likely to win ratification. This is where Nevada came into the picture and my baptism into the hot-lava landscape of controversial legislative politics began.

Nevada has a citizen legislature composed of sixty-three members who meet on a biennial basis. The ERA arrived on the docket of the 1973 legislative session at a time when Nevada was particularly suspicious of federal overreach, with the ongoing Sagebrush Rebellion pushing back against the federal control of 89 percent of Nevada's land.

There was a handful of women in the Nevada Legislature. Three of the four women in the Assembly supported the ERA, but the sole female senator opposed it, claiming it would undermine family, the cornerstone of society. Defeated 16–4 in the Senate and never voted out of committee in the Assembly, the ERA did not stand a chance in the 1973 legislative session. It would have four more chances. Its supporters would need to press forward with more might.

With more pro-ERA women recognizing the depth of opposition and scope of the challenge, a statewide coalition of supporters organized under the banner Nevadans for ERA. Working with the next legislative session in mind and in coordination with groups such as the League of Women Voters and the American Civil Liberties Union, a strategy emerged. In 1975, we saw initial success with the Assembly voting 27–13 in favor of the amendment, but in the Senate, hopes were defeated.

This simultaneous gain and loss prompted pro-ERA activists into overdrive while at the same time, the opposition ramped up their efforts. The Church of Jesus Christ of Latter-Day Saints, a formidable force in Nevada politics, began actively working to defeat the amendment at every turn. Mormon bishops throughout the state, in a departure from their traditional avoidance of political lobbying, enjoined the women in their congregations to voice disapproval of ERA language, supporters, and policies.

In the 59th session of the Nevada Legislature, in 1977, the ERA would come closer than it ever had to ratification. Because of the Assembly's support in the 1975 legislature and assuming continued support there, we anticipated a possible victory. Based on 1976 election outcomes and promises various candidates made to us, our strategy going forward was to win approval in the Senate first and then the Assembly. With clever political maneuvering that entailed the invocation of an obscure Senate rule, state Senator Joe Neal invoked Senate Rule 30, which disallows any abstentions. Therefore, the Senate's votes of ten ayes, eight nays, and two abstentions became, under Senate Rule 30, ten ayes, and ten nays, allowing Lieutenant Governor Bob Rose to cast the tiebreaking vote in favor of the ERA ratification. Pro-ERA forces, I among them, were ecstatic: victory was finally within our grasp. The celebration was short-lived, however. In the hours that followed the favorable Senate vote, the Assembly defeated the amendment. We were devastated.

The Assembly defeat shocked pro-ERA supporters, particularly given the confidence built over years of doing the groundwork, developing a base and strategy, and channeling campaign dollars to male candidates that, in turn, flat out broke their promises. The betrayal, although the toughest revelation yet, sparked even greater resolve. We would press on in the next election cycle, targeting those who had caved under pressure from leadership, which was primarily Mormon.

This is where I was drawn into the statewide coalition, Nevadans for ERA, to ratify the ERA.

As a member of the ERA coalition, and as a woman, I was bitterly disappointed and outraged that a proposition so fundamentally fair and reasonable—a proposition that ensured equality, under the law, for half the country's population—could engender such intense political controversy and hostility. The continued and obvious resistance to the ERA was eye-opening to women across the country. The outcome of the 1977 legislative session fired my resolve to put Nevada's ratification vote across the finish line.

The upcoming 1978 election was our only hope of reversing the defeats of the last three legislative sessions. As the representative of the rural north on the ERA Steering Committee, I was pressed to identify a pro-ERA candidate from my legislative district. I was dead set determined to do that. The vote to ratify the ERA might hang on my success, so I tried my heart out, reaching out to whomever I knew to suggest possible candidates. But few in my rural neighborhood supported the amendment, and those who did were not receptive.

"It's a nonstarter," they said.

"Career killer," I heard more than once.

"You know women's liberation falls into the same category as communism for many of our constituents, don't you, Jill?"

Returning to the Steering Committee empty-handed, I was told: "Then you run, Jill. If we want to succeed, we need a candidate in every Nevada county who will support ratification."

I couldn't imagine it: me, a Democrat in an 80 percent–plus Republican district that had never before elected a Democrat, much less a woman who was already known as "nontraditional" and "a rule breaker." As I explained to my fellow activists on the ERA Steering Committee, "My life is on a different path."

As a PhD candidate, I envisioned a life of teaching, research, and scholarship in a field I found fascinating—anthropology. I loved studying different cultures around the globe, particularly the Middle East, where I had spent three formative years working after college. The world of election politics was as far from my imagined future as Mars from Earth. My resistance got no nods of agreement.

"Okay then, keep looking for someone else." I tried again and failed.

Feeling boxed in and guilty for letting the team down, and thinking to myself, "This is nuts," I finally caved. "Okay then," I said. "I'll run."

In childhood I exhibited a "daredevil" streak, following somewhat in the radical footsteps of my great-grandmother, Emelie Melville—who in her childhood was a Shirley Temple-esque actor on the Broadway stage. Later, as a young woman, Emelie became a luminary in the San Francisco theater scene and in the international comic opera and theater circuit. Emelie defied late nineteenth-century norms, first, by marrying businessman Tom Derby and then by continuing to pursue a career and travel abroad without her husband and two young children. She was then also at the center of a widely publicized scandal in 1875, disgracing the well-heeled and respected Derby family into which she had married by eloping with a fellow actor to Australia.

Emelie was always known by her stage name Melville. Similarly, when I married my husband, Steve Talbot, I kept my name, my family name, Derby.

Though now a common practice with a sizeable slice of marrying women, a wife not taking her husband's family name was unheard of in the seventies, particularly in Nevada. Use of one's husband's first and last names following Mrs. was how women were identified in public listings or in newspapers—with all individual or separate identity disappearing in the designation. Departure from this norm was reserved for female movie stars or artists, and people in Douglas County and beyond frequently told me that what I was doing was illegal. Naturally, I had checked and knew otherwise. A woman changing her surname was a matter of longstanding custom, but not the law (in most states).

I believed that becoming Mrs. Steve Talbot would instantly erase thirty-three years of my life's experience as "Jill Derby" and disconnect me from the four generations of Nevada's Derby family heritage.

Steve had my heart; I wanted to keep my name.

The matter, roiling my mind for months as our relationship deepened and I became convinced that Steve was the right man for me, was decided the night of his marriage proposal. We were sitting in the J. T. Basque Bar in Gardnerville in 1972. A Picon Punch might have fueled my resolve, but the rebel in me—the one I often attribute to my great-grandmother, Emelie Melville—also bolstered my will. I raised the issue of what we later came to call the "name thing" as others weighed in on our then controversial choice. Hardly anyone—we came to discover—including our families, thought it was okay. Steve had never heard of a woman keeping her "maiden name." His previous wife, Vicki, had become a Talbot, so this was unfamiliar territory for him.

But as we talked at the bar that night, sipping our drinks, I asked a question that opened his mind further to the suggestion and sealed the deal: "How would you feel about changing your name?"

"I can't imagine it," Steve replied. "I've always been a Talbot. I'm a Talbot, that's just who I am."

"Well," I said. "I feel the same way. I've always been a Derby and can't imagine being anyone else."

"Then you stay Derby, and I'll stay Talbot, and we'll tie the knot," Steve said.

I warned him that our decision might prove controversial.

"It's our choice," he said. "We'll deal with it."

Steve's ease with defying a prevailing marriage custom only confirmed my sense of him as being his own person—someone comfortable in their own skin. He was a man's man wrestling with cattle and horses in his professional role as a large-animal veterinarian, but he came complete with a subsurface tender side, as is the case with all people who love and relate to animals. He was gender-secure and comfortable with a nonstereotypical wife who had separate pursuits and felt engaged in a larger worldview than the one that prevailed in Douglas County in the early seventies. Steve has often joked that before we were married, he had visited a total of three western states while I had traveled around the world three times, lived in the Middle East, and visited thirty-one different countries. He likes to say that he married a worldly, nontraditional woman who brings interesting conversations to the dinner table.

A look at comparative temperaments behind marriage choices is interesting. Some people choose to marry those of a similar disposition and personality, while others are drawn to a contrast. In our case, the adage that "opposites attract" carried the day.

My mother had counseled me in my early twenties when I was in a dating swirl: "Don't marry a man who wants to clip your wings; marry a man who loves the way you fly."

Her words stuck with me as an aspiration that fit, even while knowing that American men are largely socialized into a husband role of dominance and control. Steve and I both think we got the better of the deal, and that's what makes for a successful marriage. Almost fifty years and two kids later, we think we have proof we got it right.

Steve had two children by his first marriage, whom I understood came with the package. Geoff and Brinn were three and five when we married, and Steve had granted full custody to their mother, who moved to the Bay Area and later remarried. Working six days a week in a two-man practice with long hours into the night on many days, he knew of his limited time to raise children. I was commuting to the University of California, Davis, many weeks to complete my doctorate coursework and could not have helped much with children either. Also, I was apprehensive about becoming a stepmother knowing the long-standing negative literary tradition surrounding that relationship—think Cinderella and Snow White.

Our recalibrated family arrangement worked out better than most. Steve and Vicki retained a fairly amicable relationship focused on the kids' well-being, and for my part, I made no attempt to be a substitute mother—Geoff and Brinn already had a good one. I decided to be like an aunt or some peripheral relative who told them the same riveting, made-up stories my father told me as a child when I drove them over the Sierras and they stayed with us over school vacations and holidays. As for discipline during those visits, that was Steve's job. A stepmother can take on too much baggage if she takes on that role, and my goal was to build a warm and loving relationship with Steve's children. Geoff and Brinn, well-raised in their own blended family in Lafayette, California, are great kids who have done well in life. We continue to spend good times together.

Before dating Steve and entering the doctoral program at UC Davis, I spent a postgraduate year at UC Berkeley studying Arabic and Middle Eastern cultures. I had attended the university as an undergraduate and lived there before moving to Saudi Arabia.

Berkeley is a city known for its unblinking support of norm-busting social innovations connected to the human potential movement, including feminism. Most of Nevada, still tethered to the cultural norms of the fifties, was unaware that women could consider (or be considered for) any aspirational alternatives to housewife and helpmate.

To add to my outlier status, I was commuting 150 miles weekly to Davis, to complete my graduate coursework. My staying on campus sometimes for days at a time raised the ire of women in my new Nevada community. They let me know they disapproved my violation of expected wifely duties by asking, "Who is taking care of Steve?"

I didn't know how to answer their mean-spirited queries, so I didn't. I just hoped Steve didn't lose weight, which would confirm how awful I was for leaving him to fend for himself—he didn't.

Framed in this context and given the fact that even though I was a woman who many considered brave—a risk-taker—throwing my hat in the ring as a political candidate was a daring and brash move. When I said to my Nevadans for the ERA Steering Committee colleagues, "You've got to be kidding," they met me with resolve and smiles. I smiled too, part of me thinking, "This is a lark! I don't stand a chance. Oh, well. Game on!"

I knew nothing about how to tackle the challenge I had agreed to but decided I would give it my best shot. The day after agreeing to run for legislative office, I ordered five "how-to" books on running a political campaign and began to do my research. I called a few friends who shared my commitment to the passage of the ERA and asked for their help. Over the course of several weeks, we passed the books around. We each took notes and then held meetings, conferring, and making a plan.

A palpably audacious and revolutionary spirit quickly emerged among us, even though we knew how unlikely our endeavor seemed in our deeply conservative and Republican county. I had studied at UC Berkeley, and was continuing at UC Davis, but I was also a fourth-generation Nevadan. I knew quite a bit about the values that permeated ranch and cowboy culture. To top off my direct experience observing the world around me as I grew up, my dissertation research was focused on the lifeways of cattle ranchers in western Nevada.

Ranching is centered on raising cattle, but far larger and more alluring than all the land devoted to cattle grazing are the legends and myths surrounding the rancher and the cowboy way of life. Hundreds of popular novels, songs, and movies highlight a rugged, independent, hypermasculine image of the western cowboy. Rodeos across the West dramatize the range skills of herding cattle, riding horses, and roping. Daring boys and men ride dangerous bucking bulls and broncos. It is not surprising that the towns and communities around Nevada that serve the ranches in their area reflect the culture that ranching life has engendered.

Beyond the economic focus of my study, I was looking at gender and cultural norms on ranches. Cattle ranching is the "Marlboro Man's" world. Women do play vital roles in these enterprises, but the culture surrounding ranching celebrates men and their activities, those that are often idealized in fiction. In my study, men ran things; they were the bosses. Women in leadership roles were not part of the cultural picture. So, my life in politics was about to launch in a very unlikely setting.

My team and I had about eight months to put together a political campaign. The internet did not exist in 1978, so we did mainly what the how-to books told us to do. We obtained political registration information, precinct maps, and former election data and records from the county clerk's office. Doing as the "Groundwork" chapter in one of our books instructed, we analyzed these records in terms of voter turnout and election results. Getting our toes wet in the political realm offered a steep learning curve for all of us, given our zero cumulative prior knowledge of any of its machinations. Poring over maps to plot door-to-door campaign logistics, I felt a long way from my courses in Middle East cultures and could not yet see how my doctoral studies related. Nonetheless, my teammates and I persisted, fueled by the passionate righteousness of our cause—equality for women.

We engaged in all the traditional campaign activities for that era. We put on fundraisers with parking lot auctions of donated items in the middle of town. We held bake sales and sold tickets for a fall harvest moon dance. We put up signs and had literature printed, going door to door handing it out. We created and shared with everybody to whom we spoke the special "Derby's Best Recipes" booklet containing simple meals and desserts titled with political flair, such as Democrats Spinach Salad and Republican Jell-O Salad. We studied those how-to books and not missing a beat, practiced and perfected our polling, using the multiple phone lines of a dental office that belonged to the husband of campaign committee member Judy Williams. We relied on voter rolls and the good old-fashioned phone book to poll day after day as we drew close to the election.

I read and reread the chapters on how to be a successful candidate, often rolling my eyes and re-experiencing the initial "you've got to be kidding" reaction I had when my Steering Committee peers told me it was time to step up to the plate. The successful candidate, the book said, walks unfamiliar neighborhoods knocking on strangers' doors and introducing themselves. I saw this approach as incompatible with my more reserved personality. I had long considered myself a small-group person who was not drawn to interacting in large crowds. Beyond my graduate field work, I had limited experience approaching strangers with an outstretched hand, and my confidence that rural Nevadans would welcome such boldness was low.

"This isn't me," I told myself.

Being "a candidate" wasn't me before I read how to make it me. Being "a candidate" wasn't me until I went out and became one. This was a watershed life-changing realization: you become what you do, I learned.

My peers and I discovered so much in our how-to books. We learned we needed to target and start out in neighborhoods in Gardnerville and Minden that had high voter turnout in previous elections. It was time: I approached our first designated street with a campaign colleague accompanying me for support. She walked on the opposite side of the street, and I hoped she couldn't hear me muttering to myself, still, months into our commitment, "I can't believe you're doing this, Jill."

I was all-in now. I couldn't let my loyal campaign colleagues, for whom I was the team leader, down; I couldn't let Nevadans for the ERA down. Off I went.

The first few doors were daunting. I forced myself to take several deep breaths as I reached out my hand to knock, knock, knock. I arranged my expression to look as relaxed and pleasant as possible. To my surprise, I found most people friendly, semiwelcoming, and curious. Being a youngish (thirty-eight-year-old) woman, I was not a threatening sight, and nobody was ever hostile. I introduced myself, letting them know who I was and why I was there: "I'm running for the state legislature."

In response to the raised eyebrows and an "Oh, congratulations," or a neutral "Mmm-hmm," I said, "I'm interested in hearing what your concerns are in relation to state and local issues."

People liked being asked for their opinions, and I found myself interested in what they had to say. Visiting constituents door-to-door was an engaging and stimulating exercise after all. Block after block, hour after hour, I walked, knocked, introduced myself, listened, and handed each person with whom I spoke the little heavy-stock "Derby's Best Recipes" booklet. This small and useful offering turned out to be an important psychological support for me: I had something to give people in exchange for their conversation and time. I would point out a particularly tasty casserole or cake, and then I would ask for their vote. Maybe I was a natural at campaigning after all.

My graduate student training was proving to serve me well. Cultural anthropologists do their research into human groups by asking questions, noting answers, and discovering patterns in the responses. For my dissertation, I had spent weeks with Nevada ranching families. Without realizing it, I had grown into someone who was comfortable conversing with strangers. It was mostly women who were home, and sometimes retired men. A country friendliness was endemic in rural America in those years, and maybe it still is, as long as you don't wear a rainbow pin on your lapel.

The only traumatic experience I had walking in rural neighborhoods came not from people but from dogs. On more than one occasion, I was chased out of a fenced yard. I had been advised, as with bears, that running invites pursuit. I wasn't willing to test out the theory with these cattle-protecting dogs defending their territory; however, one time, I did run clear across the street to my car when a dog leaped its fence in hot pursuit. Another time, a barking dog came at me from behind a house and when I turned to escape it, the gate stuck, so I leapt that fence, tearing my skirt in the process. I learned to carry doggy treats in my pocket, wear shoes I could run in, and survey an enclosed yard for the quickest exit before entering.

Other parts of the campaign were more challenging than walking precincts and soothing country dogs. My opponent, Lou Bergevin, was a well-known member of a prominent Republican family in the Carson Valley; he expected no contest from me, a recently transplanted upstart of a young female Democrat, so there were no debates for which to prepare. Nobody in the dominant Republican Party gave me a second thought. The local newspaper, *The Record Courier*, recorded my announcement of entering the race on a back page in a short paragraph. State newspapers had made light of my efforts and ambitions as well, noting as a foregone conclusion that a Democratic woman in Douglas County was somewhat oxymoronic and not to be taken seriously.

Speaking at events was intimidating, particularly at candidate forums. I had limited depth on issues, and I continually worried people would ask me questions that I couldn't answer. My campaign theme centered on being a candidate who would listen to the people but did not go into any great depth on local and state issues.

In the middle of a candidate forum, a long-time Carson Valley Republican—and critic of mine—called me a carpetbagger. Scrambling to remember the difference between a carpetbagger and a scalawag from my high school history class, I had no immediate response. Relatively new to the valley and caught off guard, I failed to point out that my extensive Derby family connections to Nevada stretched back more than a hundred years.

Derby Dam is named after my great grandfather. At age nineteen, Thomas Derby II ventured from New York to prosper in the California Gold Rush. Although he was not a miner himself, his hard work and business acumen eventually led him to own the company stores of the New Almaden Quicksilver Mine near San Jose. The New Almaden Quicksilver mine was the largest, richest mine in California, producing more metallic wealth than any gold mine.

In the 1890s, following the advice of his younger brother, Richard Derby, who worked for the Union Pacific Railway Company in San Francisco, Thomas purchased sections of land in northern Nevada along the Reno-Lovelock corridor. Derby was initially a small dusty train stop but in 1905 became a town built to accommodate the workers on the Truckee River diversion dam project, funded through the US Reclamation Act of 1902.

Rough and tumble, the town of Derby reportedly gained a bad reputation for its frequent saloon shootings. By 1912, less than a decade after completion of the dam, the population had shrunk to about fifty. The post office closed in 1922, and the town was abandoned. The Derby Dam itself developed a similarly negative connotation, having proved lethal for Pyramid Lake's native Lahontan cutthroat trout species, which became extinct there because of the dam's diversion of the Truckee River. Given these less than sterling associations, I tended to be guarded in mentioning the family connection to the Derby Dam, particularly when in fishing circles.

That said, a recent development in the long saga of the Derby Dam has delighted the fisher community and rectified an historic injustice to the native Paiute people, who have lived and fished at Pyramid Lake from time immemorial. As a result of the dam diverting water from the Truckee River for farming irrigation purposes, over time the water level in Pyramid Lake dropped by eighty feet. In 1940, the native Lahontan cutthroat trout, a staple of the Paiute diet, was declared extinct.

Miraculously, half a century later, a small population of the fish was discovered in a small creek in Elko County, on the Nevada-Utah border. In 2006, the species was reintroduced into Pyramid Lake in an event heralded as an amazing feat of the US Fish and Wildlife Service and other biologists.

Most recently, in 2021, in an award-winning logistical and engineering achievement of considerable ingenuity and expense, a fish screen was designed, tested, and installed. The largest horizontal fish screen in the United States, it allowed the first Lahontan cutthroat trout in more than a century to bypass the Derby Dam without moving farther into waters that are too warm for its survival. With this happy development—farmers are content, and age-old fish migratory patterns are restored—the reputation of the Derby Dam has been mended, and I can now feel comfortable mentioning its connection to my great-grandfather.

Derby Field airport in Lovelock was also named after a section of land that was owned by my great-grandfather and donated by my great-uncle Howard, his son. Near the Flying Flapjack Ranch that my father and mother developed in the 1930s, and where I began life, it obviously had special meaning to me when I piloted my first solo flight, in 1975, from Minden Airport to Derby Field.

My Derby-Nevada connection does not end with a dam and an airport, I might have announced to my Republican critic.

My grandfather, Charles Derby, earned a mining degree in UC Berkeley's first School of Mines graduating class and worked as a mill supervisor in Virginia City from 1909 to 1912. My father attended grades three and four at the Fourth Ward School there, along with his older sister, Mariquita, two grades up. Years later, when I was a child, my dad pointed out their Washington Street home on a tour of the town we took when I was young. My grandparents decided to leave Virginia City after having their third child, Eleanor, because, the story goes, grandmother Mary hated the dust. They moved to Nevada City, another mining town, for the rest of my father's schooling.

When I was a child, our family drove down from Tahoe to Nevada City for Fourth of July celebrations and so that he could point out the Derby family home there. I don't remember being riveted by these tours, mostly because I was always in the back seat and often carsick on winding Sierra roads. Now, as a parent myself, I understand the lure of memory lane, and the pleasure of visiting one's childhood haunts that hold the roots of one's sense of personal history.

In the years that they lived in Virginia City, my grandparents, Charles and Mary Derby, traveled back to the San Jose ranch where Thomas Derby Sr. had retired. Their route traversed the Sierras via Spooner Pass and Lake Tahoe, where they visited the small bay of Glenbrook, where most of the timber that supplied the Virginia City mines originated. In 1937, with the inheritance Thomas Sr. left him, Charles purchased four acres on the shores of Lake Tahoe—in Glenbrook—when the Bliss family began selling off some of their holdings.

I spent all my summers growing up in the cabin that my father built there in the 1940s.

My parents decided I was part fish because after learning to swim at age two, I spent so much time in the water. My only negative memory of those glorious Tahoe summers is of our weekly shopping trips down to Minden and Carson City where carsickness plagued me on the old Kingsbury Grade and Spooner Passes with their endless hairpin curves. The drive never affected my older sister, Pam, the same way.

Another favorite Nevada childhood memory is of my time spent every summer at Camp Galilee, an Episcopal Church camp on the shores of Lake Tahoe, just a mile from Glenbrook. I met kids from all over Nevada there, and some are still friends today. I had been christened at St. John's Galilee when it was at Stateline, Nevada, before it was moved to its current location in the forties. I read recently in a small news clip saved in my baby book that George Palmer Putnam, a former publisher, husband of Amelia Earhart, attended my baptism, along with his then-wife, Jean-Marie Consigny, who had just published *Gardening for Fun in California*. No one from the ceremony is still alive, so I cannot unearth the backstory of that occasion, but I do remember my parents reminiscing about some writers and friends from Hollywood who visited their Flying Flapjack Ranch and Tahoe when I was too young to remember or be impressed.

My parents, Tom and Helen Derby, met through flying lessons my father was giving at the San Jose Airport, where he had been part owner. It was 1936, and the United States was still in the midst of the Great Depression. So to avoid the expense and flurry of a society wedding—the type that my grandmother hoped for—they eloped to Lovelock instead. My grandfather had asked my father to go and develop the family land there that he had inherited from his father.

The expense of a diamond engagement ring in those economically stressed times seemed extravagant, so my mother suggested an alternative. Once settled on the ranch, my father bought his bride a horse, a happy substitute for a diamond ring. Mom named her horse Solitaire.

My parents set for their kids several examples of flouting social tradition for more personally satisfying outcomes. They hosted many friends and family members—all curious about this pioneering, homesteading, outback adventure on which the newlywed couple from San Jose had embarked.

My dad liked to tell the story of how the Lovelock ranch got its name. He had sketched out a picture of a derby hat, a style well known at the time, and drew wings on it, choosing the moniker "The Flying Derby" ranch. As a pilot, he felt the design fit their new venture. He showed the drawing to an acquaintance in a Lovelock bar,

who exclaimed, "Hell, Tom, that's no hat. That's a flying flapjack."
The name stuck.

Between 1936 and 1943, my parents transformed the Lovelock
property from a vast empty space with a dilapidated house that had
stood vacant for six years to a livable home with cultivated fields.
The accumulated debris from desert winds had to be raked out of the
rooms. They had no choice but to make immediate improvements.
Their first week there, my mother fell through the rotted boards of
the porch while trying to shower with a makeshift device my father
had jerry-rigged. In one of the first of a long series of "Letters from
Lovelock," my mother wrote: "On the 13th, of October, we drove
up to a grey house surrounded and filled by the most unbelievable
quantity and quality of debris. I was making up a poem and asked
Tom for one word which would describe our new home. He unhes-
itatingly offered 'grubby,' and I wrote it down."

Only days after arriving, an incident occurred that my father
laughingly recounted for many years afterward. My mother wrote
it up colorfully:

> It was the third day at the Flying Flapjack and the wind blew inter-
> minably. Every gust brought a fresh supply of powdery dust where
> there was already more than plenty. By that time, I was about
> through with pioneering. I wanted nothing more than to go to a
> hotel where I could have a hot bath, clean clothes, and have my
> meals served to me, dust-proof and labor-free.
>
> As I walked to the door of the tool shed, a scene met my eyes
> that was the last straw. Tom stood in the kitchen door surrounded
> by a semi-circle of strange men. They did not look friendly. It prob-
> ably comes of being tired and of reading too many western thrill-
> ers, but I could imagine what they were saying was something
> like, "We don't want no strangers in this part of the country, see."
>
> We controlled the only stock water for miles, and I decided I
> would fight for our rights, so I rounded the house and came into
> the kitchen behind Tom, where I knew the gun was. It was .22 cal-
> iber and had all the impact of a door knocker, but it was our only
> weapon. The men finally slouched away, and Tom came back to
> me. He explained that they were neighbors, were glad we were
> here, and sought permission to use our stock well. When he heard

of my rallying to our defense, he was touched, no doubt, but only said slowly, "You must never shoot anyone with a .22. If you ever did and he found it out, he would be terribly and justly provoked."

Their marriage was off to a rugged but adventurous start, and Mom, as always, found humor and remained grounded in the practicalities of facing the challenges in desert living.

During those Lovelock years, and because of their proximity to the famous Lovelock Cave, my father's interest in Nevada archeology grew, as did his library on the subject. Dad, a UC Berkeley alumnus, connected with Robert Heizer, an archaeologist who participated in the fieldwork done on the cave.

Arrowhead hunting was one of my father's favorite off-the-ranch activities in the years before restrictions were appropriately placed on such things. Mother wrote in her letters of his finding dozens of artifacts in a single outing. Dad found projectile points, blades, scrapers, and other tools on and near their property. In the seventies, he donated his entire collection to the Nevada State Museum in Carson City, where it was on display for decades as one of the museum's premium collections. My father worked with museum staff archaeologist, Donald Tuohy, and they became good friends. Tuohy recognized Dad's avocational knowledge of archeology, made him a museum associate, and included him for several years on archaeological digs in the region.

My father, who was too old to join the armed services when World War II broke out, found a role in 1943 training pilots for the Air Force. He worked out of Rankin Field in Tulare, California. My mother, who graduated from the College of the Pacific in Stockton and had taught school before marrying, took a job teaching second grade. In nursery school, we were forced to line up for a spoonful of cod liver oil on our way in each morning. I have hated liver ever since. The only bright spot in those lean and drab war years in Central Valley's Tulare was that Mom managed to collect enough of those little red gas coupons to get us back to our cabin at Lake Tahoe for the summers.

The Lovelock ranch was put up for sale in the years that followed the war, and in 1946, we moved to Los Gatos to be nearer to both Mom's and Dad's families. Los Gatos, nestled next to the California coastal mountains and surrounded by miles of orchards that have since been paved over, was an idyllic place to go through school.

When I was thirteen, we almost returned to Nevada. My mother's fears finally persuaded my father to give up his flying career, and he accepted an offer to be the mill supervisor at the Copper Canyon mine near Battle Mountain. His college major was in agriculture, not mining. But having grown up around mines all his life where his father worked and having spent several years working in the mines of Mexico after college, he knew that world well.

My mother was teaching at the Llagas Country School near Los Gatos at the time, one of the last one-room schoolhouses in California and an historical marker featured in a 1953 issue of *The Saturday Evening Post*. I completed the final months of grade seven attending my mother's school after being expelled from the Los Gatos Grammar School for smoking in the girl's bathroom. Mom had her hands full raising two teenage daughters in Dad's absence.

While the idea of moving the family to Battle Mountain was being contemplated, there was some conversation of sending my sister and me off to the Annie Wright Episcopal Girls School in Oregon or Washington. But when hordes of Mormon crickets descended on Battle Mountain at the time of our early family visit to the Copper Canyon mine, relocation was swept right off the table.

The long thread of Derby family history spans more than a century in Nevada, and it is likely that I have deeper roots in the Silver State than my Republican critic at that long-ago Douglas County candidate forum did. I was clearly not the carpetbagger I was falsely accused of being, and had I seen the insult coming, I could have shut it down with a host of family stories.

A year earlier, I could never have imagined myself standing in a room, speaking to a crowd about my candidacy for Nevada Assembly District 39 and being called a carpetbagger. The moment I decided to throw my hat over the fence and run for state legislature, I did go all in. I went to the county clerk's office, signed candidacy papers, and paid the small filing fee. I was a woman running!

In the primaries, I had a female opponent—Bonnie Borda—who was a member of the almost nonexistent Democratic Central

Committee in Douglas County. Bonnie did not support the ERA, and so our first challenge was winning the summer primary election, which we did. Having taken on the campaign activities our collection of how-to books outlined, it wasn't hard to beat someone who was counting on winning thanks to a long association with the county party and family name recognition. Bonnie and her team didn't engage at the grassroots level like we did. By winning the primary, yes, we lost a few friends among old-time Democrats in the community; but we swallowed the social consequences, never once slowing down. Our victory provided the green light to go full throttle into the November election.

A new crew of women joined our effort to help put up signs and distribute our campaign brochure and cookbook in neighborhoods further down on our priority list. I continued my precinct-walking, knocking, smiling, and asking about peoples' concerns, mostly in outlying areas now (we were further along in the campaign, having covered many of the denser neighborhoods in town earlier). Out on these three-to-five-acre parcels, I wore flat shoes (better to cover the rough terrain and to outrun the occasional dog) and a skirt or dress, of course. This was the seventies, and women wearing pants in rural neighborhoods were either going horseback riding or out to milk the cows. My credentials were already shaky on any social scale, and dressing counter to the norm would not have won me any votes. Better to look like a friendly neighbor in approaching a doorstep.

Near the end of the campaign, we spent a week of evenings in Dr. Gary Williams' dental office, using its multiple phone lines to make down-to-the-wire polling calls. Gary's wife, Judy, was one of the pillars of our campaign team. Our excitement grew as we dialed and asked for votes. It looked like our grassroots efforts were paying off. We had far more support than the party registration profile would have ever predicted.

In the meantime, we were told by those with ears to the ground that a rumor was circulating; it was said that our campaign was being orchestrated by forces in Washington, DC! It was "too professional" compared to anything our county had seen before. We delighted at the compliment. It dawned on us that whatever the outcome, we had made a mark and were illustrating what a handful of determined women could do when energized by a cause they were passionate about. It didn't take rocket science to make significant gains, just a determined spirit, hard work, and grit.

The night of the election, we sat on my living room floor around the coffee table and waited for the results to start coming in. A supporter called and said he had heard that Bergevin had reserved the Carriage House, the largest venue in Carson City at the time, for a victory celebration. He was being joined by the who's who in county government and politics.

"We'll see," we said.

We knew what the polls were saying, and Bergevin, expecting a landslide victory, hadn't bothered to check on any predictors. Those labels I'd been given—*an unknown, an upstart, a female, a Democrat*—assured him of an easy victory in a county that had never before elected anyone who bore one of those labels, let alone all four.

The counting went on well after midnight, but just before the local television station was preparing to go off air, the news announcer said, "One of the biggest upsets of the night is that Democrat Jill Derby, in one of the most Republican districts in the state, has won election to the Assembly."

We were beyond delirious! Oh, my God. We could hardly believe that all our work in the face of so much skepticism and daunting registration statistics had actually come to this. All the neighborhood walks, all the campaign strategy sessions around our dining room tables, all the phone calls and handing out of materials by all the volunteers—replaying our playbook together, we cried in joy. We remembered the setbacks: how at our fundraising auction at the Stratton Center, a few people turned their backs when I took the podium; how someone called me a "carpetbagger" at a Service Club meeting. The utter elation of victory erased all the snubs and whispers. Our passion for women's equality nurtured a camaraderie and force that could not be crushed. We laughed and danced; we cheered and toasted!

I don't recall sleeping that night. Early the next morning, I got a call from the leader of the Nevada Assembly suggesting certain committees on which I could serve. It was heady stuff for me, this cheeky woman who had taken on the campaign as a lark.

Late the next morning though, another call came through. The absentee ballots counted in the clerk's office overnight turned the outcome in my opponent's favor by about one hundred votes.

It was shattering: this was the official result.

My campaign team and I gathered at my house and cried. We vented. We tried to get our minds around how such a euphoric victory had so quickly, and by so few votes, been snatched from our grasp. An 80 percent–plus Republican district had come so close to electing a relative newcomer, a female Democrat advocating for women's rights. If just half of those absentee ballots had been for Derby . . . but of course, those people had been out of town, they had never met me. An eight-month-long, inspired, uphill, never-let-up effort had resulted in such joy and relief; and then, within the space of a few hours, such grief. Numb with disappointment, we felt paralyzed.

The toughest aspect of an election campaign, win or lose, is when it is all over. You have poured so much heart and soul into what you believe in and hope for, you hold your breath while the returns come in, and there is so much emotion riding on it all. I won't sugarcoat it: Our near win, our defeat, was a gut punch like none I had ever known. It was so close. It wasn't fair. We deserved to win. We were up against overwhelming odds, we worked relentlessly, and our cause was just. But in the end, there was nothing for me to do but comfort and acknowledge my wonderful, loyal campaign team and lick the wounds of defeat.

I called my opponent and conceded the race.

A 2,000-year-old Chinese proverb begs to be told as this Nevada story and my life in it unfolds. It goes like this:

A Chinese farmer acquires a horse which soon runs away. A neighbor commiserates by saying, "That's bad news," to which the farmer replies, "You never know what's good or what's bad."

Then the horse returns with another horse in tow; "Good news the neighbor comments." The farmer replies, "You never know what's good and what's bad."

Next, the farmer gives the horse to his son, who rides it, is thrown off, and breaks his leg. The neighbor weighs in again: "Bad news, so sorry," to which the farmer again replies, "You never know what's good and what's bad."

The next week the emperor's men come and take every able-bodied man to fight in a war. The farmer's son is spared.

In our darkest hour of our defeat, we didn't see that a brighter future could appear. The void in the days that followed our defeat hovered in contrast to the frantic activity leading up to the election. My campaign team and I were faced with a suddenly empty calendar, signs to take down, and office supplies to disperse.

A further blow in the 1978 election was delivered to the thousands of women who lobbied for the ERA and supported pro-ERA candidates—the Question 5 referendum in which Nevadans voted against the ratification of the ERA, 123,952 to 61,768. This voter outcome was undoubtedly the linchpin of the ERA's defeat in the state. Subsequent Nevada legislatures would simply say "the people have voted" and not give the ERA ratification any further discussion.

While the disappointment of losing our race began to fade, we decided we would make good of the bad and try to learn a thing or two. What had we done that had enabled us to almost win such an uphill battle? What could we improve upon and share with others moving forward?

We obtained the precinct-by-precinct breakdown of votes and gained valuable insight analyzing the results. I had won by large margins in some of the most solidly Republican precincts in the county—precincts with zero support for the ERA. What I remembered about those precincts, some of the most rural in a rural county, was that I had knocked on almost every door where I found someone at home. I had good conversations with people who weren't used to seeing a stranger walk up their path. Along with other anecdotal information, I concluded that these people voted for me because they had met me. They liked my outreach and conversation, never mind my Democratic Party identification or pro-ERA position—which I didn't lead with but did not hide. One of the most profound aha! realizations from the entire exercise of my political campaign boiled down to this: *personal connection and likability eclipse party and policy differences.*

Time provided a salve, as did recognizing the gift of such an intense and educational experience. As the campaign dust cleared, I could see avenues ahead that would have been unimaginable before.

Having entered a whole new world of election politics, I had gained new skills, new insights, new friends, and new confidence in tackling the unknown and sticking to worthy pursuits. I had not yet officially become a student of transformational learning—this was a movement I would be drawn to in the nineties—but as many people know, the best way to learn is not though books alone, but through lived experiences, especially profound ones. The moment I, this unlikely novice, knew I was going to be running in a political race, I bought the "how-to" books. Being a candidate and putting words and concepts into action brought me new knowledge and expertise. I became a different version of myself, one that would navigate the future with a broader perspective.

When experiencing failure and set back, spiritual teacher Ram Dass urges us to "use it as something to become wise." And as the adage goes, today's pioneer is tomorrow's expert. Returning to my doctoral studies following the campaign, I knew I would find ways to put to good purpose the lessons I had learned as a political candidate. My passion for advancing women's rights though political activism was set ablaze and would never abate. Just as I knew after having my first baby that I would have a second, I knew I would run for office again someday.

In the early seventies, Bella Abzug, Shirley Chisholm, Betty Friedan, and Liz Carpenter formed the National Women's Political Caucus to work to pass the ERA and elect more women to political office. In 1979, after the fourth legislative defeat of the ERA in Nevada and my own narrow loss, a group of activist women who had worked for the passage of the ERA formed the Nevada Women's Political Caucus, a state affiliate of the national organization. I was elected the first president, with Mary Coffey, Stephanie Lamboley, and Alicia Smalley serving with me as the initial cadre of officers.

In the eighties, I would say goodbye to my mother, finish my doctorate studies, give birth to my daughter, begin traveling the world with my family, and remain fully engaged in politics. In a later decade, my initial "Who, me?" would include campaigning to a group of baffled men in a bordello café, dodging free-range cattle on a deserted highway at midnight, and driving through Nevada's Area 51. Following a late-night campaign stop in a remote area on the Nevada state border, I would drive seventy miles into Utah before discovering I had taken a wrong turn.

Those are events and adventures to be recounted later, but the rest of the ERA story is state history. The Nevada Legislature defeated the amendment in the 1979 session and did not even give it a hearing in the 1981—the final opportunity for passage within the seven-year window the states had to ratify. The conservatives had found loyal ears and triumphed, but that multiyear political struggle on the part of so many women in Nevada—women who had never engaged in political activism before the ERA—changed the political landscape of our state forever. It took time; it took resolve, but that visceral defeat of our passionate efforts to put women's equality in the US Constitution morphed into a fierce determination to put women, progressive women, in those legislative seats that had so let us down. As the Chinese farmer said, "You never know what's good and what's bad."

The betrayal by male allies we supported fueled our initial resolve and prompted us to funnel our energies into electing a state legislature that would advance women's rights, not block them. It was that crushing defeat of the ERA in Nevada that galvanized women across the state to work politically for a different future. Leaders of the Nevadans for ERA campaign such as state coordinator Kate Butler, Renee Diamond, and Cynthia Cunningham, who were leading organizers in the south, and Mylan Roloff in the north were tireless in their efforts. Harriet Trudell, Renee Rampton, Naomi Millisor, and Vivian Freeman were major figures in the campaign along with legislators Mary Gojack, Jean Ford, and Sue Wagner, and there were countless other unnamed volunteers. We lost that battle, but none of us walked away in defeat.

We were blessed with male allies too, who worked alongside us for this fairer future for their mothers, wives, and daughters—but it took Nevada women saying, "If we can't change their minds; we'll changes their faces."

We celebrated a significant milestone in our determined efforts to elect women to political office in the 1990s. In the first years of the decade, three of Nevada's six constitutional offices were held by women: Frankie Sue Del Papa, who was the first woman to be elected Nevada's secretary of state in 1986, became the first woman to be elected the state's attorney general in 1990; that same year, Wagner became the first woman to be elected the state's lieutenant governor, and Cheryl Lau became the first Asian American woman elected to serve as Nevada's secretary of state. These glass-ceiling-shattering victories by three impressive Nevada trailblazers signaled to us that we were well on our way to the legislative success for which we continued to strive.

In 2018, exactly forty years after my political initiation as a pro-ERA candidate, through extensive statewide training programs, election after election, and incremental gains and victories, a dream came true: Nevada achieved the seminal accomplishment of becoming the first-ever women-majority state legislature in the United States. We lost the ERA, but forty years later we captured the state.

CHAPTER 2

My Life before My Political "Yes"

Several personal awakenings mark the backstory of my political transition from being a supporter of Republican presidential candidate Barry Goldwater in 1964 to heading up the Nevada State Democratic Party in 2007. Mine has been a multidecade journey with many leaps, twists and turns, insights, discoveries, and epiphanies— all learning opportunities that a more traditional trajectory would not have provided.

So seriously did I take my Episcopal upbringing that I not only taught Sunday school, sang in the choir, and served on the altar guild as a young adult, but I also contemplated a calling to the religious life. Camp Galilee was my summer centering place, and in high school and my undergraduate years of college, I regularly visited a convent for silent retreats. In my senior year of college, I signed up for an Episcopal Volunteers for Mission program and considered becoming a nun!

My parents, who saw a professional future for me, were aghast at my flirting with such an option, but it wasn't their objection that dissuaded me so much as the questioning of Sister Patricia at the Convent of the Holy Nativity in Santa Barbara, California. At one retreat, she asked me to take a closer look at what truly lit me up. Sitting in silence and listening to my heart, I determined that what called to me most deeply was traveling and exploring the world.

At age twenty-five, a Mason-Dixon Line in my life's trajectory, I accepted a job as a dental hygienist with Aramco (the Arabian American Oil Company) in Dhahran, Saudi Arabia. I had planned to study philosophy at UC Berkeley, a subject that had long fascinated me, but my godfather, who was a dentist, talked me into a different career. Along with my parents, he knew of my ambition to travel and convinced me that acquiring a profession that provided independence and a good salary was a better ticket to the world than philosophy.

"You can read Socrates on planes and ships as you travel," he said.

I switched my major and between UC Berkeley and the University of California, San Francisco (UCSF), earned a degree and professional credential. After four years of practice, two international trips (the second one around the world by ship and by land), a final year on the UCSF dental hygiene faculty, and then, thanks to a strong letter of recommendation from the chief executive officer of the Bechtel Corporation (Steve Bechtel was a patient of my godfather, his dentist), I got the call. Aramco gave me three weeks to accept its offer of employment. Whether to move halfway around the world to a Muslim country was a major decision for a single, twenty-five-year-old female. The company wanted to give me plenty of time to consult and consider. But I didn't need time. I called my folks to share my excitement, and they were delighted for me. They knew and had encouraged my dreams of world travel. I called Aramco the next day and signed on.

Six months later, with a footlocker and suitcase in tow, I was off on my adventure of living abroad. A photo of my parents and favorite maternal aunt, Tante Cille, seeing me off at the San Francisco airport sits on my desk to this day.

On midnight of July 1, 1966, I landed in Dhahran, on the Arabian Gulf in Saudi Arabia. I can still remember the thrill I felt as the pilot cut the engines and prepared for our descent. A great journey had just begun, and yet, I knew nothing of what lay ahead for me.

Growing up and thumbing through the pages of *National Geographic* magazine, I had always dreamed of visiting foreign lands. I never avoided launching into the unknown. In my youth, I sought out thrills other children avoided. I rushed for the front seat of the roller coaster in Santa Cruz, California, while other kids held back, gripping their parents' hands. I leaned forward over the restraining bar with my hands in the air, shrieking with delight down every steep, scary drop on those wild, winding tracks. I liked to dive from the highest piers in Glenbrook.

My daredevil streak brought me both delight and grief. From an insight I gained at a self-discovery workshop I attended in my fifties, I was surprised to learn how ten of my closest friends and family defined me.

"What three words would you use to describe me?" I was charged to ask.

"Fearless." This was the first adjective seven out of the ten used.

Really? I might have expected "independent" or "nonconformist" and "go-for-it-girl," but not "fearless." Sure, the unknown was never a deal-breaker, but I saw myself as just busy choosing exciting options in front of me. Looking back, I can see a pattern of making choices different from those of my peers: while all my close high school and college friends got married soon after college, in several weddings I remained a bridesmaid who instead chose to launch herself onto the other side of the globe.

"That's no way to find a husband," I was told, time and time again; but world travel was more alluring to me than domestic pursuits. Besides, waiting a decade to find "Mr. Right," as it turned out, paid off in gold.

My first morning in Saudi Arabia, I was given a tour of the community and a handful of introductory literature letting me know what to expect and how to navigate the compound's layout. Like many company towns in foreign lands, Aramco was enclosed in a compound with many of the amenities of a small US town, such as a commissary, dining hall, post office, school, community center, tennis courts, and houses with lawns and palm trees scattered along circular streets. I was struck by how much it looked like home. Orientation on the second day consisted of a sit-down session with other new arrivals, where two critical rules were reinforced: respect the desert's scorching heat and respect the Saudi Arab culture, especially concerning drinking and dress.

Summer heat, regularly climbing to more than 114 degrees Fahrenheit with humidity in the high 90 percent range, could be deadly. Land Rover excursions into the desert to go "pot picking" (a.k.a. artifact hunting) along the ancient caravan routes were a favorite pastime for "Aramcons," but getting lost in the desert was fatal. Equally lethal in our host country—a conservative Muslim nation that forbids alcohol consumption—was being caught with alcohol. Expats caught drinking were flown immediately out of the kingdom, with no time to pack, to protect them from the Saudi authorities and jail.

The dress code for women venturing out into the local town called for modesty: long sleeves, pants, and below-the-knee skirts. Anything skimpier would earn a loud public scolding from the local moral police (the *mutawa*) who enforced strict Wahhabi standards.

They would also, as I was to discover one day wearing a cap-sleeve top, threaten you with a stick. It was embarrassing being yelled at in public. I had hoped to go unnoticed, but I knew the code and understood that I had violated it. Fortunately, I lived there years before the current draconian Saudi code was imposed on foreign women that requires them to wear full covering with an *abaya* and *niqab*.

I took the job with Aramco with an open mind and an interest in learning the Arab language and customs. Intrigued by the different view my new Arab friends had of family and kin, etiquette, values, and social expectations surrounding males and females, I began to more intently question, listen, and observe. I sometimes learned about differences by committing an embarrassing *faux pas,* but I mainly found that people were receptive and even pleased when asked questions about themselves.

Along with the endless process of discovery in which I was engaged, I saw how easily misunderstandings could occur simply because people look through their own cultural lenses and attach different interpretations to the same behavior or set of circumstances. It's sometimes called "culture shock," and I learned quickly that my way of seeing the world was not always how others saw it.

From the moment I landed in the desert kingdom, I was excited to settle into my new surroundings and felt warmly welcomed by those with whom I would be working. I was happy to learn that I would have time off to learn Arabic since I would be training Saudi boys who worked in the clinic. At the same time, keen to learn more of the local culture directly, I experienced a growing sense of disappointment—the Aramco compound housed mostly Americans. Furthering my language skills and cross-cultural knowledge would require my own initiative. Telling those Saudi boys that I wanted to learn their language and customs delighted them. Out of our camaraderie in the clinic came an early invitation to visit the home of Mansour, a fourteen-year-old who lived in the nearby town of Dammam.

As Mansour and I walked down the mud-baked street toward his home, curious neighbors peered from around doors. Inside, Mansour's mother and sisters were gathered in a simple carpeted sitting room with cushions on the floor, around a small table with an Arabic coffee pot, small cups, and refreshments of dates and sweets. None of the men of the family were there, of course, which would have been an unthinkable violation of the gender code—I was an unrelated single woman.

Nobody except Mansour spoke English, so he translated all conversation, which consisted of many long pauses of silence. I struggled with what might be appropriate to ask or say. The family let me know that I honored their home by my visit and continued to offer me more sweets and yet another cup of the bitter, cardamon-laced Arabic coffee that I never learned to like. I continued to drink it because they insisted despite my demurrals, and because I didn't want to risk being rude. Being a guest at Mansour's home was the dawn of awakening about how little I understood what was expected according to Arab hospitality and etiquette norms. Then, after the coffee server was empty, I mortally embarrassed myself.

On one wall hung the sitting room's single adornment: a five-by-two-and-a-half-foot desertscape painting, done by an amateur, maybe a family member. Wanting to make conversation by complimenting the piece and prompting its story, I told Mansour to tell his family that I liked the painting. When Mansour walked directly to the wall, took the painting down, and handed it to me, I thought, *What! Oh, my God. What have I done?* I was mortified. "Oh, no, no," I exclaimed. "I can't take this. I didn't mean . . ."

As I continued to stumble over more words of refusal, Mansour's mother and sisters joined in, indicating that I must take the painting. Nothing I said dented their resolve. Nothing! Leaving their home with their large painting under my arm, I effusively thanked them for their hospitality and kindness.

Offering guests hospitality and generosity is a central code of Arab culture. The custom, as I've been told, has developed over centuries of living in a hostile desert environment, where welcoming a stranger into one's tent can be life-saving. Mutual expectations around such hospitality have long served the common interests of desert tribes. As I so strikingly learned from Mansour's family, to admire something in the Arab context is akin to asking for it. For all three years of my stay in Dhahran, I kept that painting hanging in my apartment. It marked my determination to learn the language and the mores of polite behavior in the Arab world, and it served as a reminder of how limited I was in my American upbringing to navigate a foreign culture. This first major *faux pas* abroad (and it wouldn't be my last) also marked the beginning of my interest in studying different cultures.

Arab nationals from Lebanon, Jordan, Syria, Egypt, and Palestine who worked in the senior staff around me at Aramco became an important part of my circle of friends. I watched how they navigated social situations in gatherings, family visits, and other occasions. I learned to check my assumptions at the door. After several years of mind-shifting experiences, my fascination with the *what's* and *why's* behind different customs and attitudes led me to consider the idea of returning to the US, and to college, to study cultural anthropology. By learning other cultures from the inside out, I imagined, I could build links of understanding among diverse groups. I could help move the automatic human response to encountering differences in others from uncertainty and fear to curiosity and affinity. Idealistic, perhaps, but immersion in a foreign culture can have a transformative impact if one is open to the discoveries it offers.

Living and working abroad changed me 180 degrees, mentally, politically, philosophically, intellectually, and religiously. The mix of surprises, shocks, joys, and traumas in my life overseas would forge a less innocent me, but one with lots of exposure to "the other" and many lived experiences on which to reflect and question. My time visiting new places with new people broadened my worldview and sense of human diversity while whetting my appetite to understand more about the full spectrum of humanity.

The Aramco compound itself operated on its own set of standards, allowing the women who lived there wide discretion in dress, especially in the hottest months. The strict alcohol prohibition was also widely ignored, and many residents distilled their own beer or wine using equipment components borrowed from the oil drilling inventory. (The one wine I tried to make was undrinkable!) Specialty brands were rare, and at cocktail parties one ordered simply "white" or "brown" liquor with whatever mix was available through the commissary. Taking anything alcoholic outside the compound was very risky. Aramco had a lovely sandy beach cordoned off on the Arabian Gulf for swimming and waterskiing on weekends, but picnics did not include Budweiser or pinot gris.

One of the earliest American friendships I formed was with

Angus and Wylene Graham, a Florida couple and fellow Episcopalians, who invited me on some of their Land Rover camping trips out in the vast sand dune-studded eastern Saudi desert. Angus, a pediatrician at the Aramco hospital, introduced me to Dr. Azmi Jarrah, his Palestinian colleague. Azmi and I became friends, and on one of the Grahams' weekend camping trips, he and I violated Aramco's number-one hazard warning: we got lost in the desert.

It happened innocently enough: after a convivial campfire dinner, as folks retired to their tents, Azmi and I decided to take a getting-to-know-you walk out across the desert in the moonlight. What could be more exotic than strolling in the cool of the night across the dunes in the middle of nowhere? We wandered off the knoll of our campsite in an arbitrary direction completely absorbed in conversation for some time. I was fascinated by Azmi's background, which was so different than mine.

We were startled and came to a halt when a thick fog rolled in, surrounding us. Warm, dense fog was not uncommon so near the Gulf, but neither of us had experienced it yet. We quickly took stock of our location (nonlocation), realizing that the campfire on the hill that we assumed would guide us back along the same route was no longer visible. In fact, nothing was visible. We started back the way we came, only to realize after ten minutes of fast walking, blindly encased in fog, that we had no idea whether we were retracing our steps or heading at an angle in a different direction.

We stopped; I was worried. If we were really lost, we wouldn't last past noon the next day without water. We decided to stay where we were until the fog cleared, sitting and talking and waiting. Azmi taught me a Lebanese folk dance to keep me distracted. Finally, long after midnight, the fog cleared. There was no firelight in the distance, however, and we had no sure sense of which way to head, so we sat on the ground waiting the hours until morning light. What a way to get to know someone! (What a first date!)

Then a strange thing happened that was so unnerving I thought being lost in the desert with no water was the least of our problems. A small, silent light hovered in the distance. Azmi and I couldn't tell how close it was, but we immediately thought it was the Grahams coming to look for us. We jumped up and ran toward the light, shouting, "Here we are, here we are!" But there was no response. We shouted louder, but as we ran closer to the light or glow, we noticed that it seemed to be floating or hovering oddly, not like someone carrying a flashlight, not like anything we knew. Azmi and I paused in total silence. The light was silent too.

In sheer fright, my knees gave way and I sank to the ground. Azmi crouched immediately, thinking the same unthinkable thought. We crawled behind a bush, watching, and whispering our mutual fear. If what we were seeing was a UFO, it must not find us. I thought of my mom and dad never knowing what happened to me. I had never been so frightened. Within five or ten minutes, whatever that light was, it suddenly vanished. Azmi and I stayed glued to the ground behind that bush for the rest of the night. Were we really alone?

We agreed to tell no one what we had seen. Neither of us had ever given serious thought to UFOs, but we knew the ridicule those who claimed to have seen them faced. With the first signs of daylight, Azmi and I stood and stretched. Able to make out the rise of the knoll and the campsite in the distance, we hiked back, arriving early before anyone awakened. I crawled into my sleeping bag and lay there relieved to be alive and back in the safety of friends. As others stirred, I got up, offered to help cook breakfast and said nothing about the night's extraordinary adventure.

The Grahams moved back to Florida the following year, and I missed our desert campouts. Forty years later, at their daughter Megan's (my goddaughter's) wedding, I confessed to them during the rehearsal dinner the happenings of that long-ago night in the Saudi desert. To my utter astonishment, they confessed to me that they too had seen what they believed to be a UFO in that same location on another camping trip that summer. They, like Azmi and me, had told no one. We laughed and laughed.

Getting to know some of the non-American professional staff around my age—Lebanese, Palestinian, Egyptian—provided me with the opportunity to spend time outside the American bubble. Through Azmi, and later, Husayn Alami, with whom I had a close relationship, I became comfortably familiar with the different worldviews and values these friends expressed, particularly their deep commitment to family and intellectual interest in what was happening in the rest of the world. I also saw our common humanity.

The transformative impact of immersing myself in a different culture brought me the discovery that those raised in different cultures see the world through a different lens than I did. The culture shock of the desert painting incident at Mansour's home was only one of several embarrassing missteps that led me to realize that I was blinkered by the values, norms, and judgments with which I was raised. Learning to let go of the preconceptions and misconceptions I carried with me opened me up to inquiry and revelation many of my more cloistered expat colleagues missed out on; but, more importantly, it changed the way I would engage with the world for the rest of my life. Experiencing a foreign culture increased my bandwidth to learn and grow in ways classroom lessons never could.

Educational theorists have long proposed that the best learning comes from experience, not textbooks, and neuroscientists go further with claims that experience actually rewires the brain. Jarring experiences, such as culture shock, can alter the mind to whole new ways of thinking. Looking back on those flustered moments I suffered in my first year living abroad, I saw that those embarrassing times led me to realize that the mental equipment I had for making sense of situations in America didn't work in other places. I am grateful for the epiphany it provided.

My thirst for traveling with intent and purpose grew in the Middle East. From Dhahran, I could take short flights to countries on the Mediterranean and longer flights to Africa. I flew often for weekends in Beirut, and to Istanbul, Athens, and Cairo for longer visits. Famous and fascinating historical sites in Iran were less than an hour's flight across the Arabian Gulf—the ancient cities of Isfahan and Shiraz were a weekend destination.

On yearly flights back home to Tahoe, I stopped in Asia on the way, and in Europe on the return. All this travel gave me an experience of global humanity in all its variety, and a realization that people are the same the world over. Separate from their governments, many of which were not democratic and some that were more aligned with the West than others, the people in their shops, homes, and marketplaces were simply people, like me. Language differences aside, everyone everywhere shared common dreams centered on community, family, home, food, children, work, play, religious events, and traditional celebrations. Our Thanksgiving and Fourth of July celebrations, unique to Americans, find their parallels in expressions of national and cultural pride all over the world. I had the chance to partake in several end-of-Ramadan feasts and a few Eastern New Year celebrations, which usually take place later in the Western calendar year. I even shared a meal at a Bedouin encampment out in the Saudi desert and managed to avoid being offered a sheep's eye, a delicacy I didn't think I could handle with grace.

The 1967 Six-Day War occurred during my time there and while many Americans were evacuated from Dhahran, I chose to stay. I had Arab friends and wasn't ready to abandon ship. The Saudi Arab employees of Aramco staged a strike over American support for Israel in the war. Protests were threatening and protesters destroyed property, but no injuries resulted. Feelings and tensions ran high, and uncertainty reigned.

An announcement was made over the clinic intercom: we were being told to depart immediately for our residences because demonstrations were breaking out nearby. Standing at the entrance to the clinic, I could see a chanting mob at some distance. I didn't feel personally threatened, having many Saudi Arab friends who worked for Aramco, but I was ready to obey the order. As I started down the steps, I saw a familiar figure standing by the perimeter fence. Quickly, I went to him.

"Mansour," I said. "What are you doing here? A strike has been called, and you must not stay!"

In words I still get tearful to recall, he said to me, "*Anisa* Derby, as long as there is danger, I will stay and be your soldier at the gate. I will protect you."

This fourteen-year-old boy, my protector—I was speechless. Recovering my voice, I insisted he leave, but he would not move until I promised to go straight to my apartment. Rounding the back of the clinic, I looked back over my shoulder. He was still there. I prayed he wouldn't be noticed and punished for defying the strike order.

Such a searing memory of a human-to-human bond amid opposing sides in a volatile conflict forged a new understanding for me that people in conflict are just people with different convictions, people with beliefs derived from different life circumstance, people such as Mansour and me. With a human face drawn across battle lines, my sense of what an "enemy" is or should be, changed—it was neutralized. Simply seeing things differently than someone else is no reason to go to battle and destroy lives and livelihoods for generations to come. My experience of the Dhahran protests would inform my view of the war in Vietnam after my return to the States.

During those disrupted weeks in Dhahran, I was involved in many conversations—some with Palestinian friends whose families had lost homes in the 1948 establishment of the Israeli state. Husayn's sister was in Jerusalem, where a fierce battle was being waged. Azmi's brother had joined a Palestinian resistance group. One of Aramco's vice presidents organized discussion groups, during which the Middle East's history with the West was reviewed and various viewpoints were shared. These discussions helped transform a crisis into a learning experience and were the beginning of my insight into the way dialogue allows space for differing backgrounds, values, and opinions to unfold and be taken into account. My role in organizing a citizen diplomacy trip years later from Nevada to the Middle East, where our group of twelve women visited both Palestinian and Israeli groups to advocate for peace, stemmed from this profound experience in Dhahran amid that historic conflict.

With Aramco's Saudi employees on strike and so many Americans evacuated, those of us who had remained in Dhahran filled in to keep essential services for the community functioning. My assignment was managing the telephone exchange, which involved the old style of plug-in boards with a tangle of cords connecting parties. Given an inadequate ten-minute training and left to my own devices, I misconnected numerous calls and left others muttering, "Hello, hello, hello," from some source I couldn't find. The week was full of valuable lessons though. A crisis always shakes one's preconceived sense of an orderly world and offers new ways of viewing life, and one's place in it. Challenging times can also bring out the best in people, proving mutual assistance is the value that often prevails.

My second spring in Saudi Arabia, I took the thirty-minute flight to Bahrain, a former British colony where religions other than Islam were allowed expression. Having heard there was an Anglican church in Manama, the capital city, I decided to fly over for Easter weekend and attend services. As a bonus to my fun mini-adventure, I was invited by Anglican vicar Rev. Henry and his wife, Edith, to their residence after the service for tea. Later that year, when our resident British priest chose to retire, I suggested inviting Rev. Henry to apply for the position. He and Edith accepted the offer, and he became our new vicar.

The day they arrived was not as smooth as the move itself: Edith fell down the steps of the airplane, broke her leg, and was immediately taken to the hospital. Rev. Henry settled into the vicarage and the second afternoon called me to ask if I would come over and help him settle in and answer questions about our Canterbury group. I was happy to continue my role as ambassador of this transition for our congregation.

Rev. Henry asked a few questions about the residence and then suggested we sit in the living room to talk. The curtains were drawn, and soft music was playing. In the midst of some small talk, he commented, "You remind me of another Jill I knew years ago. We enjoyed listening to music together. You are equally as lovely."

He had chosen to sit beside me on a narrow sofa rather than on a matching chair on either side. None of this raised any red flags: he was a priest after all, and there is an intimacy with those who lay hands on others to heal and bless. When he suggested it would be "more relaxing" if we lie on the floor to enjoy the music, I hesitated, thinking, "Hmmm, this is odd." But I obliged. My role as the vestry welcoming representative was to assist with this transition.

When Rev. Henry took my arm, helping me to the floor, something felt off. When he took my hand and started stroking my arm, alarm bells sounded. Flooded with confusion and trying to look normal while sorting out what all the consequences of whatever I chose to do could be, I froze. This man was a priest, a man of God, a married man whose wife was in the hospital! What was happening went against all my conditioned notions of the clergy, whom I held on a pedestal of respect. When Rev. Henry moved his hand to my neck, finally an idea occurred, and I blurted, "Oh, no, I left something baking in the oven. I better run back and turn it off."

Looking disappointed, he made me promise to come right back. I promised but of course, didn't. I did call him, though, to say I had a mess to clean up and would get back when I could. I was shaken to my core and knew thereafter I would feel awkward every time I saw Edith, whom I liked. So much for the truths we cling to growing up and our untested assumptions about the way the world works.

Rev. Henry was not only violating his priestly vows but his marriage vows as well. Truth is the raw material of epiphany when the rubber meets the road, and my escape from the vicarage marked a shift in my religious beliefs.

My boyfriend, Husayn, was waiting for me when I returned. I tried to show no signs of the trauma I felt. I dared not tell him what was upsetting me for fear of his reaction and all that could unfold. He might have yelled at me for not hitting a man of God, or he might have headed back to the vicarage to confront my assailant. Neither outcome would have served my best interests or calmed my frazzled nerves. Like many women of the times, I carried on as if nothing had happened.

Those familiar with the many stories emanating from the #MeToo movement know the typical reaction to sexual aggression or assault, whatever form it takes: manage your emotions, absorb the shock the best you can, and tell no one. My story is no different. I was a respected member of the vestry, the governing body of that Anglican congregation, but I knew to keep silent. No one would believe me, my claims of innocence would raise doubts about my character, and I would be tarnished by the telling.

As an immediate consequence of this traumatic event, I avoided the early worship service. Normally, I liked to go at eight in the morning to reserve the day for outings to the beach or desert. This service was usually sparsely attended, and once I had been the only worshipper. No way did I want to risk being alone with our priest again. That decision was the first in what would become a long-term estrangement from the church.

Only years later did I come to view the vicarage incident as a kind of sexual assault. There was no violence involved, and I wasn't manhandled or raped. Yet, this senior priest in the head position in our congregation acted in a coercive and aggressive way, and I felt pressured and intimidated. As a young, single woman who traveled internationally and enjoyed making friends, I was used to unwanted come-ons, but being taken advantage of by a married priest was outside my scope of expectations.

My silence and lack of agency may seem unimaginable in current times, but I had come of age in the fifties, when authority figures were granted deference. Back then, being accommodating and nonconfrontational were part of the gender expectations for girls, which conditioned a vulnerability to male aggression. "Boys will be boys" was the popular saying, and males, for their part, were socialized to be the aggressors in interactions with females.

Women knew—like I did with Rev. Henry—that no matter how physically invasive or psychologically traumatizing a perpetrator's behavior was, speaking up would damage their own reputations, not the man's. Behavioral scientists will attest that social shaming—whether in the form of gossip, exclusion, or shunning—is a powerful behavior modification technique, one that has been used by groups and communities forever to hold members in line with whatever social norms the time and place prescribe.

In ethnographies of traditional cultures, anthropologists have described these honor-shame systems. Today's digitalized fame-shame version amplifies the effects by a millionfold, in the form of trolling, cyberbullying, and cancel culture. Indeed, the social media outrage machine shows that not much has changed in human behavior, except the vehicle for enforcing conformity to popular norms.

The activist passion that sparked the #MeToo movement stemmed from the pent-up anger of so many women who for years suffered the indignity of being personally violated but disbelieved, women who avoided taking action because the zeitgeist of the times prescribed accepting the status quo and staying in one's lane. The #MeToo movement has blasted the status quo, legitimizing millions of suppressed memories in a kind of passion that Margaret Mead describes as being generated from "the wounded flesh of experience." And yet, as evidenced by the Supreme Court's 2022 overturning of *Roe v. Wade* and of spectacles such as the *Depp v. Heard* fiasco, women cannot lower their vigilance.

When I escaped Rev. Henry's wandering hands and manipulation, I was not as emotionally distressed as many women who find themselves in similar situations might be, primarily because I did manage to think quickly, extricate myself from the situation, and stop things from escalating. It helped too that I come from an ancestry of strong women, women of a practical temperament. That said, I was shocked, shaken, and angry.

A testament to the times is that I felt I had to invent an excuse to flee the situation rather than confront this adulterous man of the cloth with his outrageous physical advances and possibly hit him over the head with the large Bible that sat within arm's reach.

It is ironic that as a member of the vestry I felt some responsibility to the congregation for this predatory priest whom I had helped recruit, but I could do nothing to prevent him from trying his lecherous moves on someone else. When I did briefly consider reporting the incident to the senior warden of the congregation, I thought of how in Middle Eastern culture, a woman's legal testimony is weighted less than that of a man. I was in the Middle East at the time, and this was a Western cultural community, and yet I knew that my testimony in this matter would be given even less credibility than a Middle Eastern woman's. What an irony!

The gender norms I had grown up with post–World War II were generally accepted without question. Girls and young women were raised to strive for the narrow roles assigned to them of courtship, marriage, homemaking, and parenting. Girls were socialized to accommodate the wishes of men and to defer to their needs and wishes. American society was homogeneous in terms of this cultural narrative, and few alternative playbooks were available to women. Rosie the Riveter, like millions of women who worked in war industry positions, accepted her limited agency to resist the pressure to leave her job when the servicemen, heroes of the American victory over Nazi Germany and Japan, returned and needed work.

The world for women has shifted since then. Women now do have agency to claim their rights with the backing of both social norms and the law. There may be a fault line, however, in the path to the future in terms of women's equality: if young people of today do not take heed of the limits and struggles in the decades before they were born, if they take their grandmother's gains for granted, forward momentum could suffer.

Like any jarring experience that causes a rapid reframing of one's foundational beliefs or worldview, it all worked out for the best. "The best," of course, is often only grasped looking back, but now I know Rev. Henry's actions opened a door for me to years of inquiry about religion in general, theological exploration, spiritual experimentation, and the meaning of faith. It led me to writers, thinkers, and clergy who envisioned a less dogmatic, more forward-leaning spirituality that is grounded in an inclusive Christianity. Without that harrowing, mind-shifting encounter, I might have rested in the comfort and security of an unquestioned faith and practice. Instead, I settled into an open, curious, and questioning state of mind.

Alfred Lord Tennyson wrote, "There lives more faith in honest doubt, believe me, than in half your creeds." According to experts of transformative learning, a "disorienting dilemma" often leads to a questioning of one's assumptions and to a reframing of one's worldview. The evening in the vicarage was a powerful disorienting dilemma that would lead me, several years after my return to the United States, to collaborate with other women who were interested in pushing back against the traditional patriarchal religious order. It would fuel my interest, too, as a member of the Nevada Board of Regents, in working to combat gender discrimination in higher education, where I knew that women students' prospects were often in the hands of their male professors.

In June 1969, I left Saudi Arabia, returning home to the summer of Woodstock, Vietnam War protests, racial riots, the moon landing, and the Manson murders. So much had happened in America in those three shape-shifting years of my absence that it felt like a different country. I was engrossed in the life I was leading as a young American woman living in the Middle East and didn't register all that was going on back home, nor its impact. Historic upheavals in the United States had resulted in a tense political mood and social divide.

The impact of reentering the life, culture, and society I thought I knew, but felt changed, left me in a state of reverse culture shock. My sense of displacement was not different from the disorientation I had experienced on the other side of the world when I first moved to the Middle East—a foreign land with different manners, language, and customs. I'd had many jolting episodes my first year in Saudi Arabia, when I felt off balance and uncertain about what to do and expect, but I hardly envisioned that same kind of psychological uncertainty when I returned to my own country and familiar landscape.

Volumes have been written by analysts and scholars attempting to account for the disruptive changes that took place in the second half of the sixties. Some point to the rigid conformity of the fifties, to which I can personally testify, as the zeitgeist against which the youth of the sixties rebelled. Many were questioning the inflexible expectations around marriage, family and career, gender, race, and upward social mobility connected to material acquisition, and an unforgiving code of strict sexual conduct.

The youth hippie movement took off in San Francisco with the "Gathering of the Tribes," as it was called, and rapidly spread to the rest of the nation. The magnetism of the San Franciscan counterculture resulted in one of the largest migrations of youth in history. According to writers who came to witness this unprecedented phenomenon, young people were coming in droves from big cities, small towns, and bus stops across the country, by whatever means of transportation they could find—often hitchhiking—arriving in decorated cars, vans, motorcycles, buses, bicycles, and on foot.

In *Slouching Towards Bethlehem,* Joan Didion refers to this era as the beginning of the atomization of the nation. The youth movement of the late sixties saw a new way forward for humanity through the embrace of love and community and the rejection of materialist values, consumerism, and rigid norms of social behavior. Didion had an interesting take: she saw the hippie phenomenon as an early sign of a cohesive society coming unraveled. The societal fracture that began in the late sixties expanded dramatically in the decades to follow, particularly over the Vietnam War and the politics of the status quo.

This major shift in attitudes and priorities did not take root in all parts of the country, particularly not in the rural middle states or the southern Bible Belt, which remained wedded to traditional values. From the tip of a wedge, the divide began in the sense of shared values that had previously marked American life. This cultural shift signaled a growing split between the conformist "normalcy" and sense of unity coming out of the fifties, and a new ethic reflected in protests and a radically different worldview. As the common values that characterized American society in the fifties became unglued, people chose to be on one side or the other.

Looking through a contemporary lens, it is hard for some to envision (or remember) just how "stuck" fifties social norms were. Television programming, in its infancy, illustrated how the majority of Americans lived, or were supposed to live, in black and white optics. My family's first small television was placed centrally in the living room and there, we watched all the same shows other families watched: family fare, quiz shows, and adventure programs. This shared menu of TV programming reinforced the sense of shared culture that World War II had ushered in. *Father Knows Best, Leave It to Beaver, The Adventures of Ozzie and Harriet,* and *The Brady Bunch* portrayed the ideal American family and life, and kids of my generation absorbed these Hollywood stories as the only model to which to aspire. We learned the rules about what fell within the bounds of appropriate behavior and what did not. Mr. Brady worked outside the home; Mrs. Brady did not. She cooked, cleaned, dusted, fixed the kids' school lunches, vacuumed a lot, and attended PTA meetings.

Alternative images and choices for individual expression were not readily available on TV until later in the seventies, when pioneer producer Norman Lear debuted *All in the Family.* Archie Bunker, the patriarchal family head and star of the show was a blue-collar bigot whose daughter was liberal. His long-haired, open-minded son-in-law, whom Archie nicknamed "Meathead," lived with the family. Each episode of *All in the Family* humorously showcased the contrasting values of the two generations and broke new ground in what was considered controversial subject matter. It's interesting that the early episodes of the show carried a suggested "mature audiences" warning, signaling that the content that might offend some audience members' sensibilities: "The program you are about to see is *All in the Family.* It seeks to throw a humorous light on our frailties, prejudice, and concerns. By making them a source of laughter, we hope to show—in a mature fashion—just how absurd they are."

The certainty I held about my perspective after coming of age in the rigid and placid fifties was deeply etched. I assumed that the conformist script with which I grew up was the only one to live by. No wonder it would take moving halfway around the world to knock akimbo my assumptions and my way of being. Exposure to different cultures and worldviews allows us to see there is no single best way to live: a foreign way of life was as good as my own.

Living in a foreign country with a new job, new friends, and a different language provided a sudden total immersion experience, like being in a 3-D movie with surround sound. While I was engrossed in my new life in Saudi Arabia, I failed to notice the tumultuous happenings in America because I was undergoing just as seismic a transformation myself. I left the United States a close-minded,

I-know-the-truth-conservative Goldwater supporter and would return a realigned progressive with an altered frame for seeing my country, the world, and my place in it.

I was glad to be home, but seeing the insularity of my fellow Americans—especially in an interior state such as Nevada—left me feeling lonely and isolated. Few people had traveled as I had, or where I had. Living as Americans do, geographically separated from every country other than Mexico and Canada, adds to our lack of exposure, interest, and foreign language competence. My new frame of reference was the big wide world, and few near me shared that perspective.

Adding to my personal and localized feeling of dislocation, the altered social and political landscape of the United States took some time to absorb and understand. I brought a new set of eyes and ears to the table. My capacity to listen to and understand divergent views had grown. My parents, both Republicans, recognized my new independence from their traditional conservative views. My father, who had trained pilots for the Air Force in World War II, like so many of that generation, saw only disloyalty in Vietnam War protests where I saw the right to decry what seemed wrong. People in the sixties were less polarized than they are now, and different views did not so easily rupture family relationships. In my family, we chose to avoid conversations that reflected our different political views and remained close.

Not surprisingly, after returning from the Middle East, I decided to head back to college to study cultural anthropology. I wanted to make sense of all I had discovered about the world and myself in those years. It was late summer 1969, and registration had closed at University of California institutions. Some good friends I knew from my Camp Galilee days invited me to stay with them in Las Vegas and apply to the University of Nevada, Las Vegas (UNLV), just twelve years old at the time. Learning that I would need a second bachelor's degree to pursue graduate study in anthropology, I applied and moved south for the year. The campus only had three buildings and an Anthropology Department of five professors, Richard and Sheilagh Brooks and Claude Warren among them. But I thrived in that academic environment, studying subjects my years abroad had left me so curious to explore and process. I earned a bachelor of arts degree in three semesters, doing an ethnography of the small community of Overton as a summer project. I then applied to UC Berkeley, where I studied Arabic for a year and took a new and innovative graduate seminar, "The Anthropology of Women." That seminar, more than any course I took after returning to the United States, opened my eyes to the underlying dynamics of gender relations. In the years that followed, the cross-cultural, comparative study of the status of women became a central focus of my PhD study and research. The life experience I now brought to courses allowed me to have a deeper grasp of concepts and theories I studied than I had available in my first undergraduate experience at Berkeley ten years earlier.

Because my experience abroad was so eye-opening and life-altering, I continue every chance I get to urge young people to travel and live overseas. In the talks I am asked to give, I reiterate my belief that whatever our governments battle over and however our cultures differ, we share a common, interconnected humanity. The philosophical shift that took place in me between 1966 and 1969 has continued to be my lodestar, guiding every choice I make in my personal, professional, and political life.

Amid the activism and advocacy in which I was involved in the eighties, I was working on my doctoral degree in cultural anthropology. I was beginning to see, too, with my fingers in so many pies, how an anthropologist's breadth of perspective was so useful to understanding human social life. My graduate research focused on western Nevada cattle ranching life and culture, and it was a slow process, particularly writing about my findings in my dissertation, "Cattle, Kin and the Patrimonial Imperative." An almost ten-year project felt excessive until I discovered that I was the first of my graduate cohort at UC Davis to complete my PhD.

I had loved the interview phase of my project, talking with ranching families, but let me first explain how I got drawn to the study of cultural anthropology in the first place.

During the three years I lived and worked in Saudi Arabia, I had the opportunity to visit a Bedouin camp on several occasions. I was fascinated by their nomadic way of life, traveling from oasis to oasis with their camel herds. The Bedouin's entire way of life was built around the needs of their camels, which provided them with food sources on which they depended. Years later, when I was weighing research project options for my dissertation study, I contemplated returning to the Arabian desert to study Bedouin life, and especially the role of women. The idea inspired me, but there were obstacles.

For starters, in the intervening years, I had married my husband, Steve Talbot, a large-animal veterinarian who was light-years less inspired than I was about the idea of treating camels in the Arabian desert. So, in concert with my graduate advisors, I put together a proposal to study and write about cattle ranching culture right out my back door, in Nevada, and to look for cultural similarities with those who herd camels, sheep, and goats in the Middle East—a stretch perhaps, but my dissertation committee went for it. Steve's relationship with ranchers whose animals he treated provided me with a legitimizing entrée into a group of rural folks whose lifeways constitute a subculture all its own. I interviewed multiple members of dozens of ranching families over a three-year span.

I knew from my previous studies that groups who make their living herding animals have a strong masculine bias. Men who do the fundamental work of managing livestock, and the ways of life stemming from this basic male role, reflect this patricentric bias. In the western Nevada ranches I studied, men own and run ranches, sons inherit ranches from their fathers, and the women who marry ranching men move away from their families of origin to reside on their husband's family's ranch and take care of domestic needs. Often these ranches were composed of extended families built around male relationships: fathers and sons, brothers, and male cousins. Cattle ranching, in short, is a man's world.

The symbols of cattle ranching—boots, spurs, lariats, and cowboy hats—have a romantic, exotic cast to them. These symbols, deriving from the work tools and clothes of ranchers, conjure up identification with the heroes of the westward expansion and the taming of the frontier. These symbols reflect an image of a rugged masculinity and life in the outdoors, a life of self-sufficiency, physical challenge, and freedom with which many like to identify. The globally recognizable image of the American cowboy, idealized beyond the true sweat and grit of a cattle herder to a heroic symbol, has spawned thousands of books and movies and a whole genre representing manhood. Magnified a hundredfold from its frontier roots, the image of the cowboy riding the range presents a romanticized portrait untethered to reality but treasured by generations who delight in this uniquely American folk story.

In stark contrast, the western frontier of the United States was rarely a welcoming place for women, except prostitutes.

One of the main questions I pursued when talking with female members of ranching families was how they fit into their hypermasculine environment and what roles they played on the ranches. Their strategies, in pursuit of carving out a place of value and respect, ranged from taking on the role of an indispensable domestic helpmate, to participating in outdoor cattle-centric work such as calving, branding, castrating, tagging, medicating, and herding. The latter double-duty option, which involved riding out with the men, still carried the responsibility of meal preparation for male ranch workers and other supportive domestic duties. Some women spoke of riding back home early after a morning's work with the men and cattle to prepare lunch, cleaning up after the meal while the men took post-lunch naps, and everyone riding out again. This "domestic helpmate *plus*" option was not an easy choice for ranch women. But riding horses and rounding up and managing cattle are the most valued, fun, and respected activities associated with the ranching way of life.

In my dissertation, I reported the results of many interviews with women and was proud to shed some light on the figures who often did more than half the work but got a fraction of the glory. I covered other aspects of ranching life as well, touching on the prominence and popularity of rodeos in the West and how the associated danger exemplifies and promotes the value and myth of cowboy courage. I wrote on the conflict that can arise in ranching families around the issues of succession, since breaking up ranches into smaller land parcels is not economically viable.

I brought to light the pressures on ranching families and their land as population growth and town expansion offers less labor-intensive ways to prosper. I discussed the decline in working family ranches that competition from corporate ranching and "prestige ranching" has brought about. Despite the hard work involved in ranching, from early morning starts, feeding requirements, midnight calving, winter weather hazards, and the uncertain profits that depend on yearly cattle prices, most ranchers take great pride in how they choose to live. They love the outdoor focus of their work, the independent nature of their lives, and the way their heritage is idealized and treasured in American cultural life.

It took many years from the time I entered graduate school to the day my family and friends cheered as I walked across the stage to receive my doctoral hood. Writing my dissertation was a juggling act between raising my two young children and keeping my hand in multiple political activities. Much is written about whether women can have it all, and I say of course we can. It takes a supportive husband or partner, some sharing of domestic tasks, and the spark and flow of energy that comes from opportunities to make a difference in the community and the world. Women, with their inclination to consultive leadership and the use of soft power, bring a much-needed perspective to the body politic. Let's elect more women and bring a healthy gender balance into the halls of policy and power.

CHAPTER 3

All the Doors That Opened

My unplanned foray into politics, on the shoulders of having worked in the Middle East in the late sixties and having immersed myself in a graduate program in anthropology in the seventies, brought about unexpected invitations. Although I had missed the chance to serve in the Nevada Legislature, many more opportunities to advance the cause of women's equality would come my way, opportunities even more influential than a seat in the Nevada Assembly might have provided. As the adage goes: when one door closes, another opens.

With my education and experience known, I was asked to participate on panels and make presentations at conferences. In a 1978 Las Vegas conference during which I led a "Women Worldwide" workshop, I highlighted the factors that gave women higher status in some societies than in others. My goal was to raise awareness about the barriers women faced no matter where they resided.

In December 1977, the year before my political campaign in Douglas County, a *Gardnerville Record-Courier* headline read: "Local Woman Attends National Women's Conference." That was me! A budding cultural anthropologist, I was invited to participate in a State Department–sponsored Women in Development Conference with thirty women representatives of developing countries from Botswana to Bangladesh. This conference was held in conjunction with the historic National Women's Conference in Houston, Texas, that drew thousands of women from all over the country.

Our daylong Women in Development meeting focused on the impact of US foreign aid programs and policies on the lives of women. At that time, our foreign aid programs primarily invested in men, a policy that was to be adjusted as evidence mounted from meetings such as ours in Houston about the central role women in developing nations play in the economies of their communities and families. The experience of that conference led me to want to do more to advance the status of women globally. I told the *Courier* reporter that these events in Houston were "where the action was for women in 1977, and that's where I like to be."

In 1978, I could not have known that my adjunct faculty position at Western Nevada College (WNC) would foretell my leadership role on the Nevada Board of Regents, initiating a gender equity audit of all Nevada's colleges and universities leading to systemwide reforms. In a course I taught at Sierra Nevada College in Incline Village, I focused on women's strategies in various cultures to exert political influence and power. I highlighted Arab women and how despite appearances, they do have power, and they know how to exercise it from within.

I could not have foreseen that showcasing Nevada's higher education gender equity initiative at national conferences would lead to an invitation to serve as a consultant to other colleges and universities through the national Association of Governing Boards of Universities and Colleges, eventually achieving senior fellow status in the organization. I could not know a door would open to me in 2016 to become board chair of the American University of Iraq in Iraqi Kurdistan. I had no idea what might follow on the heels of my candidacy for political office in Douglas County. Much did, in terms of leadership opportunities to advance the cause of equal rights for women and support other positive developments in the world of higher education.

In 1979, following my election loss the year before, I spoke at the Douglas County Women's Caucus on the historical significance of women's reproductive freedom. I had helped found the Douglas County chapter and was elected chair. Our Douglas group consisted of about twenty-five members and remained active into the nineties. More than two decades later, a small group of us started the Douglas County Democratic Women. It has grown in stature, influence, and membership to more than one hundred members in one of Nevada's most conservative counties. In the late seventies, our goal locally and nationally was to change the statistic that women constituted 52 percent of the United States population but held less than 7 percent of elective offices. The latter number is now in the double digits, but we still have a long way to go for parity.

By 1979, I had become known in the community and region and was occasionally sought for comment. When our local paper ran the article "Mormons Anger Feminists," I was cited defending Sonia Johnson, a fifth-generation Mormon who had been excommunicated from the church for heading the group Mormons for ERA. Of Johnson, I said, "We commend her courage and her integrity for continuing to speak up for what she believes in the face of efforts to intimidate her into silence. Johnson is not the first woman to pay dearly on behalf of the women's rights movement, and she probably won't be the last. Social justice has never been won easily."

Shortly after my campaign in 1978, Governor Mike O'Callaghan appointed me to the Judicial Selection Commission, a body that pre-screens candidates being considered for judicial appointments. I saw my role as ferreting out candidates' views on the women's rights issues being newly raised in the legal system. Later, in the eighties, I would be appointed to the Nevada Supreme Court task force investigating gender bias in the state's courts. We found significant bias, with a wide-ranging impact on women, and wrote specific recommendations to address it.

Gender bias was a major focus of mine, and I saw that a central factor in the discriminatory landscape was the absence of women in the legislative, judicial, and policy bodies that determined their fate. Addressing this imbalance was where I wanted to put my energy and passion. Thus, shortly after my near-successful campaign in 1978, I turned my efforts to training other women to run for office. My qualifications came directly out of my own experience as a candidate. I teamed up with former state senator Jean Ford in offering workshops to prospective women candidates. Shelley Berkley of Las Vegas, who later served fourteen years in the US Congress, recalled that she got her political start by attending one of our training workshops in her first run for the Nevada Legislature.

Victoria Riley, executive director of the Nevada Trial Lawyers Association, and I later formed D & R Associates, a business focused on leadership training and professional development for women. We sought to enlighten participants that "through social conditioning, women have learned patterns of speech and style that reflect weakness, deference, and lack of authority."

Victoria and I trained women to analyze their style of communication and self-presentation with the goal of being heard and respected in public settings. While most of those with whom I partnered in training candidates focused on campaign strategies, tactics, and tools, I focused more on what it took to be an effective candidate—because by most accounts, I had been one.

Our training workshops, such as "How to be Taken Seriously in Male-Dominated Political Spaces" and "How to Achieve Credibility as a Woman in Male-Centered Orbits," elicited big-time *aha!* moments in participants. I pointed out embedded speech patterns and ways of being that were particular to the ways girls are raised in American society, and that detracted from them being seen as leaders. Women learn as young girls to add "tag questions" to declarations, for example: "The weather is nice today, don't you think?"

Discarding these unconscious mannerisms to take on a more confident tone and presence takes practice. Being demurring, polite, and accommodating were all considered feminine attributes. Over-smiling and over-apologizing "helped" girls and women avoid coming across as assertive, direct, serious, commanding, or God forbid, confrontational. And though nothing was wrong with women being feminine and gentle in social interactions, in public and political settings, qualities traditionally seen as feminine were not effective in convincing voters that women could hold positions of authority.

In our workshops, we addressed the relationship between body language and women's chances of being taken seriously. To underscore the role that the nonverbal signals of posture and bearing conveyed, I pointed out an example of a friend who had helped with my 1978 campaign. After undergoing multiple back surgeries that resulted in a fused spine, she walked slowly, in a deliberate manner, with very erect posture. At a crowded event we both attended, I saw her enter, and I watched heads turn. Multiple guests whispered and murmured, "Who is she?" suggesting that she must be someone important. Posture alone makes a statement. My friend walked like the Queen of England, and no one questions the queen's authority.

To highlight the influence of voice and register on a convincing presence, we referenced a study done following World War II, when women were being replaced in the workforce by men returning from combat. Radio networks explained to women that audiences couldn't associate serious news reporting with a female voice. Although women had taken over such roles while men were off fighting, they were now being informed that softer, higher-pitched voices were appealing in romance, but not effective in male-dominated spaces such as board-rooms, legislative chambers, and newscasts.

We found video to be a useful tool to help women recognize the ways in which they were undermining their own ability to sound knowledgeable and convincing. Today, thousands of studies and publications address women's speech and offer more direct and "assertive" ways of being in the world, but Victoria and I at D & R Associates were ahead of the curve and found a ready and receptive audience.

In the spring of 1979, women in northern Nevada who had fought the good fight to advance women's equality and ratify the ERA formed the Nevada Women's Political Caucus (NWPC). I was elected its first state chair. The focus of NWPC in recruiting, training, and electing women into political office influenced our determination to link arms with the National Women's Political Caucus, established in 1971.

The Nevada Women's Political Caucus was an amalgam of three existing activist groups: Reno's Anne Martin Political Caucus, the Carson City Capital Women's Caucus, and the Douglas County Women for Political Action.

The Anne Martin Caucus was formed as a support group for women who were interested in running for political office in the early seventies. Established by names now well known in Nevada political history—Barbara Bennett, Mary Gojack, and Maya Miller—the caucus was named in honor of the founder and first chair of the History Department at the University of Nevada, Reno. Martin was president of the Nevada Equal Franchise Society early in the century, and she established a press bureau in Reno to supply the state's forty-five newspapers with suffrage news in the years leading up to the ratification of the Nineteenth Amendment, which gave women the right to vote. An organizer of the National Woman's Party, Martin campaigned unsuccessfully for the US Senate in 1918 and 1920.

Bennett went on to be elected mayor of Reno, and Gojack to the Nevada Assembly and Nevada Senate. Miller, with Ruby Duncan of Las Vegas, headed up a Nevada coalition with national influence that focused on advancing the rights of women on welfare. Miller, a northern Nevada icon of advocacy for women's rights, ran unsuccessfully for the US Senate in the mid-seventies.

The Carson City Capital Women's Caucus, organized and led

by Pat Bates, Mary Coffey, and Pat Potter, had its origins offering awareness workshops for women.

The Douglas County Women for Political Action, which I had helped form and lead in 1975, was the third group to join the Nevada Women's Political Caucus. In the fall of 1979, the Bird Wilson Chapter, chartered in Las Vegas under the leadership of Laura Past and Harriet Trudell, joined forces with the three northern chapters to give the organization a truly statewide focus.

In the summer of 1979, our cadre of newly installed NWPC officers traveled to Cincinnati for a meeting of the National Women's Political Caucus. At this event, Coffey of Carson City, Stephanie Lamboley of Reno, Alicia Smalley of Douglas County, and myself, as the state chair, mingled with Bella Abzug, Lynda Bird Johnson Robb (former president Lyndon Johnson's daughter, who was the current head of the President's Advisory Committee for Women), and other national leaders.

We dashed from one political skills workshop to the next and returned to Nevada reenergized to get women elected and bring gender balance to Nevada's political landscape. Speaking to the *Record-Courier* about the event, I said, "Unlike many business and professional conventions where meetings are fitted in between tours and cocktail parties, this was all business. Women are serious about the barriers that face them and know that to overcome them requires commitment and hard work."

We had to be serious; we knew we were taking on the centuries-old tradition of total male dominance in politics and life.

We never would have dared to dream that those early learning experiences and organizing efforts would result in our state having the first women majority legislature in the United States, in 2018, less than forty years later.

The Nevada branch of the National Women's Political Caucus took every opportunity to educate Nevadans about the disadvantaged aspects of women's lives that had been kept below the surface of public awareness for centuries. Consciousness-raising was happening across the country as informal groups sprang up to read and discuss, among other breakout feminist bestsellers, Betty Friedan's *The Feminine Mystique*. Consciousness-raising was clearly needed in general, but also to counter the anti-ERA claims that things were fine the way they were, and that feminism was anti-American. As an organization committed to the advancement of women through political action, we established an annual Women and Politics Conference in Nevada that attracted well-known feminist speakers and became a yearly "go-to" event, from 1980 to 1992, in many women's circles.

Three themes I particularly pressed to include in our programs, both at the state and local levels: effective candidacy in the face of feminine stereotypes; the global perspective on women's challenges; and women's spirituality and patriarchal religion. In one panel I led, titled "Feminism and Patriarchal Religion," I drew on my graduate studies and elaborated on the proposition that when the female principle is incorporated into religious structure, language, and symbolism in other cultures, women occupy a valued and respected position in society.

Sonia Johnson, former president of Mormons for ERA, and Judy Vaughan, a Roman Catholic nun and feminist coordinator of the House of Ruth, sat on this panel with me and shared their exile and rebirth tales. Among the many other notable and distinguished speakers we brought in were Gloria Steinem, then editor-in-chief of *Ms.* magazine, and Jill Ruckelshaus, White House assistant and head of the White House Office on Women's Programs. Keynote speakers included Midge Costanza, assistant to the president for public liaison in the Carter administration, and Marilyn French, author of the *New York Times* bestseller *The Women's Room*. Shirley Chisholm, the first African American women to be elected to Congress, and Abzug, one of the founders of the second wave of the women's movement, graced us with their wisdom.

At our 1985 conference, Matthew Fox drew a large audience. Fox had authored eleven books and was director of the Institute in Culture and Creation Spirituality at Holy Names College in Oakland, California. Having fallen out of favor with Joseph Ratzinger (the Roman Catholic cardinal from Germany who later became Pope Benedict XVI) for questioning the doctrine of original sin (Fox preferred "original blessing" instead), for his alternative feminist theology (Fox called God "Mother"), and for not condemning homosexuality, he was expelled from the Dominican Order. Fox went on to be ordained into the Episcopal priesthood and write many more books.

Throughout the eighties, while President Ronald Reagan changed the nation's political trajectory, the NWPC grew the annual attendance at our Women in Politics conferences by inviting luminaries to speak on topics such as Economic Justice for Women, the Politics of Women's Health, Women in the Criminal Justice System, Gender Bias in the Courts, and Global Feminism. As we shifted into the nineties, our success was highlighted by the number of women in elective office in Nevada, which stood in sharp contrast to the gender profile of the legislatures of the 1970s that had defeated the ERA. Our success, ironically, diminished the ranks of leadership in the NWPC by the fact that most of our caucus leaders had moved on into elective offices. In school boards, city councils, the legislature, and other statewide offices, we had a solid record of success in Nevada.

We held our thirteenth and last Women and Politics Conference, "Moving Mountains," in November 1992. The title of this conference referred to the lift required to advance issues central to women's equality. Miriam Shearing, to be Nevada Supreme Court justice, was our lead speaker, and Maggie Tracey, chair of NWPC at the time, introduced the daylong session at Harveys Resort at Lake Tahoe. Tracey had served as the state chair of the Campaign for Choice, the 1990 ballot initiative Question 7 that succeeded in enshrining into Nevada law protection for women's reproductive right to abortion. Unbelievably, women still must move mountains in this regard.

In November 1977, the year before I was asked to run for office in Douglas County and before my involvement with NWPC, I attended, along with more than twenty thousand women from around the country, the National Women's Conference in Houston. I had been invited to participate in a US State Department conference held conjointly. It was this journey to which I referred as being "where the action was for women" when interviewed by my local newspaper, the *Record-Courier*.

Between the plenary sessions at the main venue and the breakout sessions elsewhere, I was exposed to the most exhilarating and inspiring voices on political organizing and activism of the era. The most thrilling moment for me though, the one seared into my memory, was physical, visual, and electrifying: I had run over from the event I was attending to watch the arrival of the torch, which had been carried by runners from Seneca Falls, New York, the site of the first American Women's Conference in 1848, to Houston. As the torch circled the arena, "The Battle Hymn of the Republic" played. The crowd, covered in goosebumps and crying tears of joy, roared.

For me, a recent transplant by marriage from Berkeley to ultra-conservative Douglas County in rural Nevada, an environment hostile to the idea of women's liberation, this event was balm to the spirit and the spark for an unstoppable commitment to the feminist cause. I wanted to capture the magic of that moment and carry it around forever. I wanted that torch to keep circling the arena of my head and never go out.

First Lady Rosalynn Carter's words to me were another highlight. Following her speech rallying support for the ERA, she exited the platform and greeted those in the front rows, where I was sitting. When I told her I was from Nevada, she responded, "We are all rooting for you out there." The whole time I was in Houston, I felt high off the energy, camaraderie, and buoyant spirit.

Returning home to Nevada, I was immediately reminded of the obstacles we were facing when Janine Hansen, an alternate delegate to the National Conference and a vocal ERA opponent, suggested in print that more than half of the women at the conference were lesbians. In 1970s rural America, that false charge had the intended negative impact. I pushed back in my press account of the conference, but as in current times, fake news and "alternate facts" were believed and left their mark.

Before the Women's Conference that year, Nevada, under the leadership of former state senator Jean Ford, convened a Nevada Women's Conference in Las Vegas in June to elect delegates to go to Houston. Steinem was the keynote speaker, and I led a workshop on the discrimination faced by women around the world. After having lived and worked in the Middle East for three years and returning to the US, I became acutely aware of the provincialism of Nevadans and the limited sense most Americans have regarding people in distant lands and cultures. Given any opportunity to share my global experience and cross-cultural insights, I took it.

I took my three-week-old son, Ryan, to that conference in Las Vegas. I was a nursing mother, and I was determined to expose my son early on to the worldview that women could do anything and everything, anywhere. It was never difficult for me to merge the joy of motherhood with the joy of activism. From the moment of delivery, I knew I could and would juggle commitments to family and to politics. In my 1978 Nevada Assembly campaign, toddler Ryan, at one-and-a-half years old, rode in the Carson Valley Day Parade with me in a vintage car. He wore a T-shirt that read, "Vote for My Mom." Women are creative, multitasking engineers and can make motherhood and politics work together.

Another feminist adventure I took was in July 1978 to Washington, DC, to attend the National ERA March. I was in the midst of my campaign and feeling the weight of the anti-ERA voices in my home state when my friend and UC Berkeley sorority sister Sally called. "Let's head east," she said. "And march!"

More than one hundred thousand women and men from around the country marched that steamy 90-degree day. All the women wore white, a tradition since the suffrage movement. Sally had made us purple and gold cummerbunds, which were also symbolic. National ERA leaders fronted the march, carrying a banner with the words of the proposed amendment printed on it: "Equality of rights under the law shall not be denied or abridged in the United States or by any state on account of sex."

I returned to my political campaign fully recharged for the months ahead and with the anthem of all large feminist gatherings at the time, Helen Reddy's hit "I Am Woman," ringing in my head.

Reddy's song brought cheering women to their feet every time it played, and I had a particularly strong memory of standing up for myself and that song at a pivotal moment in 1975. It is a diversion from politics, but a story of showing my feminist colors—which I usually reserved for supportive settings—in an unwelcoming environment.

I was in graduate school at UC Davis at the time and doing the weekly commute that so many of the women in my conservative Nevada community found unconventional and unfitting for a married woman. I had packed up my belongings from the apartment I had rented for the semester and was getting ready to head out for the three-hour drive over the Sierra Nevada mountains when I heard on the radio that a major winter storm was arriving sooner than expected. Seven feet of snow was on the way, as were 90-mile-an-hour winds. Frantically hoping to beat the storm over the 7,500-foot pass, I threw my clothes, bedding, and last batch of kitchen items into the car and dashed off. I was low on gas but afraid of allowing the storm to get ahead of me. I sped from the Sacramento Valley toward the foothills, as dark clouds, wild winds, and drenching rain rushed in.

Inching my way up the mountain pass mile after mile in a blizzard with zero visibility, all I could make out ahead of me were two glowing taillights, indicating where the road was. For hours, I followed the dim beacon of those lights. For hours, I listened to the link of chain from my snow chains that had broken loose slap, slap, slapping the side of my car. Even more catastrophic was my driver's side windshield wiper: it had snapped off under the weight of the heavy snow. As the broken metal arm etched an arc into the glass, I became terrified that my windshield would crack, shatter, and fall into the car—along with an avalanche of snow—so I turned off the wipers.

With visibility totally obscured and thinking frantically, I grabbed a spatula from the box of kitchen utensils I miraculously had with me on the passenger seat. I opened my window and with my arm hooked at a 90-degree angle, began hand scraping—with my mittenless hand—the windshield with the spatula. Snow blew in the open window. Shivering in the cold, I pressed on. My slow, lurching progress up the snow-covered grade was in a car with a floor gear shift and a clutch transmission, adding to my driving challenge and escalating my stress.

And then the car in front of me slid off the road.

Without my pathfinder ahead of me and fearing I might drive off a cliff, I stopped. If there was anyone behind me, I couldn't tell. An hour earlier, the radio announcer had said that the road had been closed in both directions. It was dark and cold in my stalled car—and utterly silent.

The only relief I had found in the hours so far, crawling my way through the center of an unfolding blizzard, was in speaking into the tape recorder I kept in the car to send audio letters to by best friend, Dru. I recorded these letters regularly on my commute, and now, on the scariest drive of my life, I was learning the value in having someone to speak your fears to. All the stress in my jumbled head poured out into the microphone. Mile by mile, I narrated the details of the swirling, cold calamity of deepening snow on the road, the loss of visibility in whiteout conditions, the banging of the broken tire chain, the etching of the snapped-off windshield wiper, and my chillingly feeble spatula solution. I described to Dru the hulking ghosts of other cars that had slid off the road before me and the faint taillights that alone signaled where the road might be, and their disappearance. Through chattering teeth, I told her how cold I was driving with an open window with snow blowing across my hands gripping the steering wheel and then settling in my lap. I kept talking to Dru because it gave me something to do in a disaster over which I had no control.

In my hurry to leave the Sacramento Valley, I had not stopped to get gas: less than an eighth of a tank remained. As the car became covered in snow, I sat alone in the dark wondering if I would be found. I closed the window but could not keep the heater running because of the carbon monoxide danger, so I wrapped myself in blankets from the bedding in the back seat and waited. I spoke into the tape recorder, telling Dru, "This might be the last anyone will ever hear from me."

Hours passed. At my lowest point, sitting alone in the cold darkness, the future seemed impossibly bleak. I vowed that if I did make it out of the blizzard alive, I would stop at the first lighted structure, get out of my damaged vehicle, hole up wherever I was, and wait for rescue.

I was running on emotional fumes when finally, I heard a loudspeaker announcement through the storm: "Highway Patrol here to rescue stranded cars."

Oh, my God, what a relief! I might survive after all. A voice said that a patrol car would follow a snowplow and lead stranded cars over the top of the pass and down the mountain. With visibility still near zero, we were told to follow the taillights of the car ahead. *Got it!* Turning the key in the ignition, I hoped I had enough gas to get to the top of the pass. If I made it to the summit, I could coast down. Again, I used my spatula to clear the snow from the windshield, and again, cold heavy snow blew in. Praying that whomever I was following had the good sense not to drive off one of the 1,000-foot cliffs I knew existed—white-knuckled and shivering—I inched my way down into the Tahoe Basin.

As soon as I could, I pulled off the road, closed the driver's side window, got out, and headed for the lights of the Rough and Ready Bar. Who else would be open at one in the morning.

Stomping my feet as I entered, I counted a couple of people inside. Blowing warm air into my cupped hands, I asked to borrow a coin for the pay phone and called Steve, who was frantic. I told him where I was and that I was never getting back in that igloo on wheels. "I'm happy to be alive, and I'll wait here for you."

Flooded with relief that I had survived a ten-hour ordeal through the biggest blizzard to hit the Sierras in years, I planted myself on a barstool and waited for rescue. I was lifted when the jukebox lit up and on came Reddy's song. A man sitting at the other end of the bar yelled out, "Turn off that goddamn song!"

Coiled tight and without a thought that it might start a barroom fight, I banged my fist on the bar and yelled back, "Don't you dare, that's *my* song!"

The bartender shot a look at each of us, chose not to intervene, and the song played on as I sang along with the refrain.

In the heyday of "I Am Woman," when old belief systems and political structures unfriendly to women's voices and power were being questioned, I found myself positioned to bring leadership and direction to women in Nevada. One area that had been prominent in my life, the church and what I termed "the challenge of the pews," struck me as an important place to open a dialogue for reform. The path of advocacy for change had begun for me in politics, but ultimately, led to another dimension of life where women were limited to a second-class status: religion. My personal journey from traditional Christianity to giving lectures about reforming the patriarchy is a winding tale of the erosion of innocence, the questioning of historical "truths," and trust in epiphanies.

Religion or spirituality is a cultural universal: some form of its expression is found and practiced in every human society. Relevant to the topic of women's equality, I learned that in societies where women played a central role in religious practice and where the female principle was incorporated in ideas about the eternal, women had higher status and greater agency. I came to understand and support the feminist effort to change the language of worship and conceive of the divine in gender-balanced terms. This, of course, raised traditional hackles, but also inspired me to act.

Given my long and complicated relationship with the church, parsing out the various injustices toward women in religion drew me in spiritedly. I had participated in the Episcopal Church since childhood, and as a young woman had begun reading books written by feminist theologians, writers, and other trailblazers of faith, who were calling into question aspects of the patriarchal structures and beliefs of the institutionalized church. One of the personal grievances I had carried for years was that only boys could be acolytes. The same sense of injustice came from the fact that in most traditions, women could not be ministers and priests. I felt strongly that the role patriarchal religion played in the subjugation of women was just as central to the fight for equality as economic, legal, and cultural barriers. Much that has changed over the past fifty years can be attributed to the pioneering women of faith who demanded a place at the altar.

When given the opportunity to direct attention to the subject of women and faith in 1983, I introduced it into the agenda of the Annual Women and Politics Conference that the Nevada Women's Political Caucus sponsored. My leadership position in the caucus gave me a platform for bringing speakers and panelists to Nevada. As previously mentioned, I hosted the panel "Women and Patriarchal Religion," which included Johnson, the ousted Mormon and civil rights activist, and Vaughan, the nun with a doctorate in religious social ethics from the University of Chicago. By speaking out on the ERA, Johnson had endured public and painful social isolation from family and friends; and Vaughan had embedded the emerging scholarship of feminist theology into the long Judeo-Christian tradition of prophets and prophecy.

Women's circles, also sometimes called consciousness-raising groups during that era, were formed to welcome, support, and educate women who were being exposed to a new narrative about gender equality. Women's circles were not a twentieth-century invention: their common purpose, whatever their time or place, was in bonding, sharing experience, and creating rituals that supported and inspired women participants. Some circles created their own agendas, goals, and ceremonies, while others fashioned themselves after sources ranging from Buddhist, Hindu, or Indigenous cultures. Since humanity's earliest beginnings, the moon has been associated with female energy. Carson Valley's semisecret Moon Circle, which I helped organize in the eighties, fit this tradition and was clearly countercultural and renegade, given the time and place.

There is a strong bond between people who share and advocate for a common cause, such as gender equality, in a majority culture that is set against such "dangerous" ideas. Friends in our Moon Circle were not go-to-lunch-and-share-stories-and-gossip friends, but colleagues in a pursuit for a more soul-fulfilling world. These were friends among whom we were free to be ourselves and with whom we could express our sense of frustration in a safe space of authenticity.

In a sea of conventional churchgoers, members of our Moon Circle somehow found each other. We shared leadership and chose to gather monthly in conjunction with the full moon. Our purpose included exploring spiritual expression in other traditions. While similar gatherings were taking place in Berkeley and other urban settings, for women like us, in rural conservative America, we felt an extra rush in our creativity, learning, and daring. We met in careful places, outside in warm months. We participated in Native American drumming and guided meditation; we invented rituals for personal passages such as divorce or relationship endings of other sorts. Candles and incense were burned, but we used no mind-altering drugs. Our goal under the moon's glow was to provide an intimate, safe space for sharing and validating personal struggles, discoveries, and soul-restoring spiritual experiences.

Two of our members were midwives at a time when midwifery was considered outside the mainstream and somewhat suspect. One member was Wiccan, one Buddhist, and others of us, Christian. We were semisecretive about our group, careful not to arouse the suspicion and opprobrium we knew it would receive, with inevitable "witchy" inferences. Some of us brought our young kids along. I did once, to our summer solstice celebration, and this led years later to a funny incident reflecting how secrets get invented and how gossip modifies facts.

Conscious always of needing to maintain an aura of respectability in the political and professional roles I was assuming, I guarded my image for the sake of protecting the credibility of my activism. In 1986, Soroptimist International of Carson City had conferred upon me a regional Woman Helping Women award for which I was deeply honored. I was being invited to speak at various clubs and forums, and when leading a social revolution, it is better not to give the opposition culturally ignitable ammunition. I never spoke publicly about our Moon Circle.

It was funny then, that about a decade after we had "folded" and my daughter was in middle school, a friend of hers made a reference to our monthly gatherings that she had heard from her mother.

"Mom," my daughter said one day out of the blue, "did you used to belong to a cult?"

It took me a moment to imagine where the notion came from: my daughter's classmate's mother was a friend of a friend of one of the midwives in our Moon Circle. In small communities, rumors travel: "Jill Derby was a cult member." I thought this was really funny. Over the years, my progressively grounded kids and I would laugh whenever they responded to some random prompt, "Oh, was that back in your cult days, Mom?"

A later and less exotic way of challenging the established religious order occurred when a few of us convinced the sympathetic priest of our small Episcopal church in Minden, where I worshipped, to agree to hold a service affirming the role of women in the context of the Episcopal liturgy, substituting prayers and hymns. I helped to prepare the service, carried the cross during the processional, and gave the sermon. Unfortunately, I didn't save a copy.

Women led the service, of course, and I have a photo of the processional that shows just a few empty pews. We promoted the service among our feminist colleagues in surrounding communities and had an enthusiastic attendance. We found inspiration and guidance in designing the service from materials that were becoming available from Catholic nuns and other women in religious roles who were resisting the extremely patriarchal nature of Christian liturgy by creating alternative forms of worship. We changed the words of hymns as gender inclusivity required. We read a passage from the Gospel of Mary, one of the noncanonical gnostic gospels more recently discovered and translated by Elaine Pagels. We read passages from Saint Julian of Norwich and Benedictine nun and polymath Saint

Hildegard von Bingen, both medieval Christian mystics who called for a more inclusive spirituality. Organizing such a gathering felt a bit audacious to a "cradle Episcopalian" who had participated in a lifetime of traditionally male-led services and who had yearned to be an altar boy in her early years.

To be honest, my revisionist tendencies ran long and deep. A bit of an outlaw whenever it came to following rules or dictums that seemed suspect and ungrounded, I had already taught my children the Lord's Prayer, altering the opening phase to, "Our Father *and Mother,* who art in heaven." Our kids grew up attending church service reciting the prayer this way, which often turned heads and invited strange looks from those in the pew ahead.

As a graduate student at UC Berkeley, I once attended a large interfaith feminist ceremony in the quad. Author and activist Chellis Glendinning led the gathering along with other women who were becoming prominent in the movement of reclaiming patriarchal faith. Later, when I sat down to help write a more women-friendly liturgy at Camp Galilee—the Episcopal Church camp on the shores of Lake Tahoe where I had been a child camper and counselor and later attended with my own children at family camps—I conjured the spirit of the women I knew in my Moon Circle and the women I admired and learned from at a multitude of women-centered events.

Although much of my exploration around religion and spirituality was rooted in natural curiosity and in recognition of the incredible range of beliefs taught and practiced globally, I had of course begun to call my own faith into question after my experience at the vicarage with Rev. Henry. In the late sixties, girls and women operated within a much narrower range of acceptable behavior and voice than they do today. Calling a man of the cloth out for inappropriate sexual conduct was not an option I felt I could exercise.

In the 1970s, the growing awareness of the lack of law enforcement support for rape victims led to the first establishment of rape crisis centers and safe houses for women victims, but sexual harassment continued to be seen as a normal part of the culture. Because it did not entail physical violence, it was something women "just had to put up with."

In *The Handmaid's Tale,* a dystopian story in which women are controlled by the state and relegated to forced pregnancies and producing offspring for a totalitarian society, Margaret Atwood reminds us: "As all historians know, the past is a great darkness, and filled with echoes. Voices may reach us from it, but what they say to us is imbued with the obscurity of the matrix out of which they come; and try as we might, we cannot always decipher them precisely in the clearer light of our own day."

At a time when many conservatives and evangelical Christians continue to espouse separate and unequal gender norms of centuries past, the #MeToo movement and younger generations are continuing women's ongoing quest for justice. Vulnerability to sexual harassment, rape, and domestic violence has been part of the female experience throughout human history. While the trajectory of progress in women's rights has been on a steady curve upward for the past century and a half, many today are asking if this trend is about to change. We may have entered an era of setbacks as evidenced in the US Supreme Court's reversal of *Roe v. Wade* and a women's right to control of her own body. Those of us who lived in a darker era, when abortion was against the law and women sought dangerous solutions to unwanted pregnancies, are worried that a younger generation of women take women's rights for granted. Unaware of the fierce resistance met every step of the way, they might not take up the fight until more is lost.

In 1981, when I was invited to serve on the Douglas County Domestic Violence Advisory Board, I did not hesitate. I wanted to work on solutions for women in difficult and dangerous situations. Violence against women has been around since the dawn of time; history is full of stories of bruised, broken, and abandoned women for whom men were the problem, not the solution. As recently as 1980, research showed that marital rape was legal in forty-four states, cohabitant rape in fifteen states, and date rape in five states.

Given today's ongoing struggle to address domestic violence, it can be hard to assess and appreciate the gains that have been made. A heightened consciousness blossomed in the 1970s over the various ways women were victimized by entrenched, stereotypical attitudes about their proper place in society. Their dependency on men for protection and support was seen as a natural outcome of female biology and feminine proclivities. Countless tales of the toughness and resourcefulness of women pioneers in the West and elsewhere notwithstanding, cultural attitudes reflected the view and interests of the dominant group, men, from time immemorial.

Domestic violence had always been considered a private matter, none of the business of those outside the battered and terrorized family. Abused women had little recourse for protection, support, or redress. The long historical record shows that Roman law gave men the absolute right to discipline their wives through beatings with a rod or switch no larger than a thumb in circumference; hence we have "the rule of thumb." Wife beating was accepted in medieval Europe and endorsed by the church as benefiting the spiritual good of wives. In the eighteenth century, British common law, following the "rule of thumb," allowed a man to chastise his wife with a stick.

In the United States, the legal tide began to turn in 1871, when Alabama and Massachusetts passed laws declaring wife beating illegal. Laws are important, but as human rights advocates have long observed, enforcement is where the rubber meets the road. It took a century of struggle for such laws to be enforced and begin to have an impact. Cultural resistance often intercedes to defeat the good and the right of laws.

The nation's first battered women's shelter was established in St. Paul, Minnesota, in the early seventies. The number of shelters across the country quickly grew. Oregon became the first state to pass a law mandating arrest in domestic violence cases in 1977. The US Commission on Civil Rights formed the National Coalition Against Domestic Violence in 1978. Domestic violence hotlines and Domestic Violence Awareness Month were also established.

When I first became involved in the domestic violence advocacy effort in my county, I found resistance to the idea of government involvement in giving women an alternative to staying in their homes and working things out with their abusers. Shelters were controversial. In Douglas County, we were ultimately able to overcome the suspicion of outside interference into domestic affairs, which is characteristic of rural culture, and establish a shelter. Similar efforts had been successful in Las Vegas, Reno, and Carson City.

In retrospect, it might seem surprising that these advocacy efforts took hold at all in a rural and conservative county. Las Vegas and Reno, with their large, urban, more educated populations would be expected to be more open to progressive change. But many of those who supported our domestic violence shelter campaign had earned their stripes advocating for the ERA in the preceding years, including many who helped with my political campaign. The failed ERA campaign ignited women's resolve to address and fight against future inequities wherever they existed. A small, dedicated group, even in rural out-of-the-way places, can have an outsized impact. "Never doubt that a small group of thoughtful committed individuals can change the world. In fact, it is the only thing that ever has," anthropologist Margaret Mead wrote.

Several formerly abused women bought their victim-honed resolve to our effort to end domestic violence as well. Mead, whom I studied in graduate school, had something to say about that development too: "Injustice experienced in the flesh, in deeply wounded flesh, is the stuff out of which change explodes."

Women in the 1970s and 1980s witnessed that kind of explosion; some of us helped set it off. I was asked to serve on the Nevada Supreme Court Gender Bias Task Force in 1987. Bias against women in the courts was one element of the "normal" order of things within a culture based on male superiority and dominance. Decision-making in the justice system was often based on stereotypes about the nature and roles of women and men, and mistaken beliefs about the economic realities of both sexes. Judges and lawyers were almost entirely men. Before the 1970s, few women were allowed to attend law school, where the path to the judicial bench begins.

The focus on gender bias in the legal system was launched in the early eighties after publication of an issue of *Trial* magazine devoted to the topic of women and the law. The New Jersey Supreme Court Task Force on Women in the Courts initiated a state-by-state movement for gender justice in the judicial system in 1983. When the New Jersey Task Force released its findings, the *New York Times* carried a front-page article entitled "Panel in Jersey Finds Bias against Women in the Courts." As a follow-up, women lawyers and judges in states around the country began requesting their chief justices to pursue similar investigatory efforts. The National Conference of Chief Justices convened a session on gender bias in the courts in its 1986 biannual meeting, following it up with a resolution urging every chief justice to establish a task force addressing this issue.

Areas of discrimination uncovered by these task forces around the country included divorce, child support, domestic violence, rape, damage awards, sentencing of juvenile and adult women, and the treatment of women professionals in the judicial system. This last area of focus was a strong incentive for the women lawyers and judges appointed to the Nevada Task Force to vigorously look for and expose areas of discrimination over which a curtain of silence had long existed. No such effort had ever been made in the courts, certainly not one with official authorization.

So it was, that in early 1987, Chief Justice Charles Springer initiated the Nevada Supreme Court Task Force for Gender Bias in the Courts, and commissioned it to:

> Consider the literature and studies regarding the existence and extent of gender bias in the country generally, and specifically to examine the judicial system of the State of Nevada to determine whether there are statutes, rules, practices or conduct that reflect gender bias and to document gender biased discrimination. The task force shall issue and provide the court with a report containing their findings and recommendations based on their study and shall provide a plan for the education of the bench, bar, and public with respect to its findings and recommendations.

I suspect that Justice Springer hoped our report would be measured and restrained, not too critical of the existing structures and procedures. The Nevada court system, like most in the United States, was overwhelmingly a male domain with a well-entrenched "good old boys' system." As the leader and shepherd of this investigatory process into possible gender bias, Springer likely felt a responsibility to his male peers to manage the final report so as not to stir up too much critical judgment or pressure for change. Stir up and press for change, however, we did.

Our Nevada Task Force consisted of three women attorneys: Kathleen England, Kathryn Landreth, and Margo Piscevich; three male judges: John McGroarty, Earle W. White, and Llewellyn A. Young; and one female Justice of the Peace, Deborah Agosti. Three of us came from outside the judicial system: former state senator Jean Ford, *Reno Gazette-Journal* editor Rollan Melton, and me.

The charge to "consider the literature" was right down my lane as a graduate student writing a dissertation at the time. A literature review is a key element in any study to provide context. In the case of gender bias in the courts, we had the advantage of reviewing the reports of other states that had preceded us in this inquiry. Two books published in the mid-eighties and written for a popular audience further informed our understanding, pointing out real-time cases of the current inequities of the justice system and the life-wrenching consequences to women's lives. These books were *The Divorce Revolution: The Unexpected Social and Economic Consequences for Women and Children in America* by Lenore Weitzman and *A Lesser Life, the Myth of Women's Liberation in America* by Sylvia Ann Hewlett.

With the help of a private firm, we conducted a survey of the perceptions of active attorneys and judges of Nevada. We placed ads in newspapers around the state to invite members of the public to send written comments to the task force, and we conducted hearings in both Reno and Las Vegas to listen to litigants and their attorneys regarding their experience in the courts.

Other state task forces focused attention on the myths and stereotypes surrounding women that bias judicial proceedings. We chose to focus instead on the concrete—more on what people "do" than what they "think." We also chose to narrow the scope of our inquiry to focus on the matters of substantial injustice in which some achievable remedy could be recommended. Because the task force's time and resources were finite, we decided to limit our inquiry to injustices suffered by women (recognizing the possibility of bias against men), and to omit the critical topic of rape of women, which we determined to be so serious a matter that it deserved a separate and singular treatment of its own.

Given these constraints, we chose three topics to address: Justice for Women in Divorce Cases; Justice in Protection of Women Victims of Domestic Violence; and Just Treatment of Women in the Legal System.

Several of the women took the lead in writing the final report. We divided up the sections to be written in draft form, and I chose to work with the group focusing on the bias women encounter in divorce proceedings. The revelations that had come to light not only in Nevada, but throughout the country, were deeply troubling. I, having married at a more mature age (thirty-three) with an evolved feminist consciousness and having chosen well in the spousal department, had not had the traumatic experience of divorce, but friends had. Hearing and reading direful accounts from many women we interviewed, I became a passionate advocate for much-needed reform.

Evidence that came before the task force revealed that the standard of living for mothers and children often crumbles following a divorce, while the prospect for fathers often improves, which did not sound like justice to me.

We highlighted the economic injustice women homemakers suffered because their work in the home was not valued in the determination of accrued assets and a fair division of property. Half of marital assets, in any case, cannot compensate for the fact that in many marriages of that era, the husband's earning power was the most significant asset. Alimony was rarely awarded, we discovered, and too often when it was, it was poorly enforced. Divorced women with children often ended up living near the poverty line. It was not unusual for a woman to have to forgo her own education and career to support her husband's education and career, only to find herself thrown back into the workplace with limited skills, experience, and opportunity for advancement.

The failure to support and enforce adequate child support was widespread. In 1984, at the federal level, the Child Support Enforcement Amendment was passed, requiring that child-support guidelines be established to bolster enforcement. At the state level, however, enforcement was inconsistent, and major challenges remained to ensure that child-support funds that were awarded were being paid.

Even in the actual court proceedings, we discovered, women were being severely disadvantaged. Statues in many jurisdictions directed judges to award appropriate interim fees for counsel and expert testimony to the economically dependent spouse, usually the wife. Judges often disregarded this directive, we learned. Our Nevada report described women as dependent spouses undergoing divorce as having to "beg the court for the funds to defend their rights, while husbands spend freely from community funds for their own legal needs."

The overwhelming gender disparity in the judiciary and the lack of women on the bench at all levels were major factors underlying the gender bias in divorce decisions adversely affecting women. As men (and judges were mostly men), their natural disposition was to identify with the position of the husband. It is easier to relate to those whose life experiences are parallel to your own: an unconscious bias perhaps, but the discrimination that women faced was more rooted in the individuals making the judgments than the institution of the court itself. The recommendation we put forward for more women judges was squarely rooted in that reality.

Justice Springer, to his credit, chose to entitle our report, "Justice for Women." It had been eye-opening to him, and he became an advocate for reform. We issued recommendations for the many areas of deficiency we found in the Nevada court system, which if implemented, would provide greater justice for women in court proceedings. We made a broad recommendation for educational programs for Nevada judges regarding the economic realities faced by a majority of divorced women, including the costs of raising children, maintaining a household, and the realistic employment and salary expectations of women given the wage inequities between men and women. Similarly, we recommended that judges in spousal support awards should consider discrepancies between the earning power of spouses, especially in cases in which the earning power of the husband had been enhanced by the mutual decision that the wife remain in the home managing domestic responsibilities.

In line with these two recommendations, we advised that judges should consider requests for permanent spousal support for older divorced homemakers with limited employment opportunity to earn retirement benefits, and that judges should give due consideration to requests for spousal support to divorced mothers who prefer to remain at home with young children until they reach school age. We stressed all these considerations involving the vulnerability and common disadvantage of divorced women in recommendations we made concerning the division of property. We also issued a recommendation regarding child support awards and enforcement, particularly strengthening the enforcement provisions, including wage withholding and jail time in hardened cases of nonsupport.

We issued a slate of recommendations around our second area of interest: Justice in Protection of Women Victims of Domestic Violence, which our inquiry revealed to be a problem of dramatic proportions in Nevada. We advised that the legislature establish laws to protect victims of violence and introduce the participation of lay advocates to support them. We called for the education and training of police, judges, and attorneys on prevention and remedies. We recommended that when independent evidence of violence existed, cases as a general rule should be prosecuted to conviction and sentencing. What seems obvious now in the fight to protect women from violence in the home is rooted in a resolve to act in the face of a problem that dates to antiquity and Rome's "rule of thumb" law.

In terms of the Just Treatment of Women Participating in the Legal System focus, the women members of the task force ensured that we included recommendations that would help right the multiple wrongs that were offensive and degrading to women participants in the court system, whether as litigants or professional personnel. We called for what is known as "sensitivity training" in other settings, pointing to insidious ways disrespectful conduct is expressed in language and slights often unnoticed and tolerated. We also recommended amending the Code of Judicial Conduct to cover misconduct related to gender bias to include discipline in cases of persistent violation.

Finally, we recommended a continuation of the task force to follow up on progress toward the implementation of our recommendations and the establishment of subcommittees with expanded representation to support the task force in carrying out its goals. None of this ever happened. We on the task force advocated for our report's widest broadcast, distribution, and presentation around the state to highlight its findings and recommendations, but that didn't happen either, or it happened to a minimal extent. I suspect the revelations of significant bias against women in the Nevada justice system and the recommendations to address it were not welcome in every quarter. The male-dominated judiciary in Nevada, comfortable with the status quo and not generally sympathetic to the strong reformist tone of the report, kept our good work from getting much attention.

Let's face it, speaking truth to power doesn't produce change overnight. But by pointing out clear bias and inequities, many of the reform efforts made in the seventies and eighties set the wheels in motion. Having seen the layout of a more level playing field, women were not willing to go back to subordinate and disadvantaged roles and positions—a theme that Reddy's "I Am Woman" song makes clear. Progress is not linear. Disappointments and setbacks are frequent, but as Martin Luther King Jr. said, "The arc of the moral universe is long, but it bends towards justice."

Other opportunities I had in the eighties and nineties to lend my voice for progressive change all came from my blinkered leap into campaign politics in the seventies. The past often only makes sense in retrospect, and I see now that my tendency to choose possibility over doubt and uncertainty, in pursuit of a beaconing future, is what made a difference for me. The opportunities that followed to bring initiative and leadership in certain Nevada quarters have arisen directly from that reckless decision I made in 1978 to throw my hat in the ring and launch into the unknown.

Living in conservative Douglas County meant many challenges and adjustments for me. I was not the first person to move from one part of the country to another and encounter social and cultural differences from where one formerly lived. As a new resident of the Carson Valley, after being raised in the Bay Area, living in Berkeley and the Middle East, and traveling globally, I needed to gauge the surrounding social temperature, weigh the ease of fitting in, and see if and where I could find kindred spirits. Moving to rural Nevada came with my marriage, so the option of moving on to more compatible shores was not an option. We humans have a natural tendency to want to fit in and find others who share our values and worldview.

For some time, I engaged in a strategy of finding reasons to bring together people who might share interests in topics of national and international concern. I had heard about the eighteenth-century French movement of creating a space in parlors for intelligent conversation on important topics, but it was an article in *Ms. Magazine* that inspired me to host my first salon in the nineties: "How to Revive the Endangered Art of Conversation and Start a Revolution in Your Living Room."

I wasted no time in putting together a flier inviting people from various lists I had assembled to consider participating in a salon or hosting one in their own homes. I called the nascent group the Carson Valley World Affairs Forum and received a positive response from about fifteen people. The first sessions took place in my home. We ate potluck style and decided on a process of rotating topics and hosts. We also chose to use the Native American tradition of the talking stick, whereby a speaker holds a stick while talking without interruption from others and then passes it along to the next speaker. These gatherings were a lifeline for many of us who enjoyed the intellectual-social engagement and shared concerns extending beyond the Carson Valley and Nevada.

One of the advantages of stepping out into the public eye is that it can draw others who themselves feel outnumbered and more comfortable keeping a low profile. A memorable opportunity I had to discover that there were more like-minded allies with their heads down than I could have imagined occurred years later, about 2003, when a handful of us in the Carson Valley decided to form a Democratic women's group. We put an ad in the newspaper announcing the gathering and set out twelve chairs at the appointed time and place. Thirty-five women showed up. One after another of the women stood up in that jam-packed living room of Julie Joldersma to announce their surprise and delight, having thought themselves the only Democrats in all of Douglas County. Our second meeting doubled the number of attendees, and thus the Douglas County Democratic Women (DCDW) became one of the most vibrant groups in the county.

In the early nineties, the Soviet Union was breaking up, the Balkan War had begun, Los Angeles had exploded following the Rodney King verdict, Nelson Mandela was elected president of South Africa, and the Rwandan genocide had taken place. For me, engagement with a small but accessible community of concerned and action-oriented individuals who were in our world affairs salon was nurturing and sustaining, much like the Moon Circle had been.

About the time the US invaded Kuwait in what became known as the First Gulf War, I helped form another community organization called the Bi-State Coalition for Peace. Our group was labeled "Bi-State" thanks to members from the adjacent California county of Alpine, who were veterans of the Vietnam protests and were committed to advocating for international diplomacy and peace instead of military action. My years of living and working in the Middle East had left me with a sense of global focus and connection to that region particularly. I had been disappointed coming back to the States and discovering how Americans tended to find the nearest new shopping mall more interesting than what was happening around the world. Our newly formed coalition was one antidote to that malaise and insularity. We invited speakers, explored topics, issued press statements, wrote letters, offered conflict resolution training, and generated actions relating to our convictions over the course of several years.

As Madeleine Albright, former secretary of state, once said, "In an era of bluster and bombs, citizen diplomacy is a builder of bridges."

Citizen diplomacy connects citizens from different countries for person-to-person dialogue that reflects alternate worldviews and helps build bonds of understanding across ethnic, cultural, linguistic, and political differences. Cross-cultural face-to-face encounters lead to the recognition of our common humanity. Citizens engaged in direct communication with "the other" experience an opportunity to learn, empathize, and move beyond the stereotypes that are often portrayed in highly publicized events and conflicts.

One of the outcomes of the peace focus of our Bi-State Coalition and our chosen focus on the Israeli-Palestinian stalemate was a citizen diplomacy trip to the Middle East. I helped organize this two-week mission in the spring of 1992, and twelve of us from northern Nevada went—five of us members of the Bi-State Coalition for Peace.

Our trip was organized under the auspices of the Middle East Council of Churches and the Earthstewards Network of Washington State, an international network for conflict resolution and citizen diplomacy. The goal of the trip was to visit Jordan, Israel, and the occupied territories of Palestine to learn about the intifada—the Palestinian popular uprising against Israeli military occupation. We flew from Reno to Amman, where we were scheduled to meet with Jordan's Queen Noor for an orientation to the region. Our team leader, Leah Green of the Earthstewards Network, gave us training in citizen diplomacy and a briefing about the conflict situation, the many meetings we would attend, and protocols of dialogue in a diplomacy context. Listening was considered central to effective diplomacy and the intent to grasp the speaker's point of view.

After our briefing in Jordan, we drove through Israeli checkpoints into Jerusalem and from there into the occupied territories of Palestine. In Jerusalem, we met with Israeli human rights and peace movement leaders as well as ordinary citizens. Following that, we had numerous opportunities for overnight home visits and a chance to spend informal time with families who gave us insight into the experience of life under military occupation. Several members of our delegation spent one night in a Palestinian refugee camp, where at some late hour they were jolted awake by an Israeli military raid. It was an upsetting incident and although nothing serious resulted, it was a first-hand experience for our citizen diplomats of what life under military occupation is like.

On another occasion, five of us were inadvertently assigned an overnight visit with a family in Ramallah that was not expecting quite so many guests. We shared a delightful meal and conversation and then were shown our bedroom with only a single queen-sized bed. We drew straws over who should sleep on the floor but later all ended up in the bed after hearing distant gun fire. I had been sworn in as a Nevada regent the year before, and one of my travel companions and housemates that night, Helen Jones, was a University of Nevada, Reno, faculty member. As she carved out her spot in the bed, she remarked, "I've never slept with a regent before."

The five of us laughed more than we slept given the logistical challenges of fitting onto a queen-sized bed—and the sound of the distant gunfire.

Our group met with peace activists in Israel after visiting a Holocaust museum, and we stood in a vigil with Israeli Women in Black, who every Friday protested the military occupation of Palestinian territories by their own government. We participated in a workshop at a Jewish-Palestinian settlement and peace school called Neve Shalon/Wahat al-Salaam. Our ten-day visit made our easy lives in northern Nevada seem trivial, complacent, consumer-driven, and self-focused by comparison. On the flight home, we discussed the enormous respect we had gained for the everyday heroes working for peace and justice in a stressful and dangerous conflict zone.

After returning home, we looked for opportunities to publicize our experience. We booked speaking engagements and wrote articles for our local newspapers. Finding a receptive audience was gratifying, though we often had difficulty finding the language to communicate our experience because it was so personally powerful.

Much has been written about the importance of a sense of community to human health and happiness, and of its decline in America. Nineteenth-century French sociologist Alexis de Tocqueville, in his famous treatise on *Democracy in America,* admired American individualism, but warned that a society of individuals without collective cohesion could become atomized. In *Bowling Alone,* written by sociologist Robert Putnam in 2000, the decline in bowling leagues in the United States is used as a metaphor to highlight the overall decline in civic participation groups such as PTAs, the League of Women Voters, and Masonic and Elks clubs. Putnam's thesis is that the loss of social connection via community groups has led to a sense of isolation and a fragmentation of society, with mental health implications.

Victor Turner, another prominent sociologist and religious scholar, claims that "at the center of all human relationships is a deep longing for shared meaning and connection."

The quest for shared meaning, connection, and discovery is what motivated me to travel globally, to observe and try on new ways of seeing myself and the world around me. The desire for connection and common cause energized my outreach to others to build communities of common interests and personal connection. Those connections have enriched my life a hundred times over.

Once you throw your hat over the wall and make the choice to step out from the crowd, the choice to champion a cause and organize groups, gatherings, and events, the rewards are multiple and satisfying. Thereafter, rising to the occasion becomes your natural response and part of who you are as a citizen activist out to make a difference in your community and beyond. As in any new role, you expand your repertoire of strategies and capacities to meet the challenges—transforming yourself and the world around you in the process. The first "yes" is what opens that door to a life of rewarding contribution.

CHAPTER 4

Three Terms as Nevada Regent

Running a good race against the odds takes heart. Whether you win or lose the campaign, you gain respect and support beyond Election Day. For me, running for office in 1978 was a bit like coming home after my first trip abroad: I knew right away I would do both again. In 1988, the right opportunity presented itself, and I was ready to jump in.

Nevada's Board of Regents is the governing authority for the state's higher education institutions, and regents are elected according to a set of districts. There were nine elected regents at that time; the district that represented my area was a five-county, mostly rural, and Republican district. The woman from Carson City, JoAnn Sheerin, who was stepping off the board at the time knew of my political background and suggested that I run for the seat she was vacating.

It might not have occurred to me to run for this office, but two factors piqued my interest. The universities I had attended, three in all, were governed by a board of regents to whom I had been writing checks for many years. I assumed they controlled the budget and were at the top of the authority hierarchy but didn't know much else and was curious to learn. More importantly, I considered education a top priority, personally and for the greater good of society. My parents, both college graduates, had reinforced their values upon me; and, the many courses I had taken, from Economic Geography and Italian Literature at Berkeley to Early African Kingdoms and Culture and Personality at UNLV, had expanded my horizons a hundredfold. A position on the Board of Regents would give me a say in how things were done in higher education across the state of Nevada. That appealed to me.

Regents (or "trustees" as they are called in many settings) are the governing authority over colleges and universities in the United States. Although boards have traditionally operated in the background, they have the final authority when it comes to major decisions and directions over institutions of higher education. In Nevada, the Board of Regents derives its authority from a provision that was written into the Nevada Constitution when it was established in 1864. The success of a university or college president often depends on their relationship with the regents—this is not a mystery. One of the primary responsibilities of the board is to hire, evaluate, and if necessary, fire a president, and therein lies considerable power and influence.

Regents, as do education boards of all stripes, straddle the space between the campus and the town square, or the "town and gown divide," as it is commonly known. Board members are citizen members of their state. They are expected to represent statewide interests while alternatively being charged as fiduciaries with the safe keeping, mission advancement, and well-being of the institutions they govern. This governing role is always a balancing act, and whenever public pressure and politics mix, the duty to protect the institution should take precedent.

The principle of having lay members of the public as the final authority governing our colleges and university was established early in our republic, to keep politics out of the classroom, where it might exert influence on what students should and should not be taught. Most countries around the world put government representatives in charge of education, but in the United States we confer that authority on citizens who put their names forward to serve on the boards through political appointment or public election. As in any political process, the outcome is as good as those who are selected to serve and is dependent on their understanding of their role and responsibility to the educational missions they are charged to protect and advance.

At the heart of the prestige of American higher education, which draws students and faculty from all over the world, is its mission of independence from political influence and pressure, along with the richness and diversity of the curricula offered. Vital to the greatness of our colleges and universities is the sanctity of a free learning environment and a marketplace of ideas where a broad range of theories, concepts, inquiries, and views are welcome. We can train students in practical, technical, and professional skills, and do, but a functioning democracy depends on an educated citizenry whose members are able to deliberate and think critically about opposing ideas. It is increasingly crucial in this age of social media influence that citizens recognize the difference between fact and fiction, data and spin, scientific theories and groundless conspiracies.

In the United States, colleges and universities seeking accreditation must go through a voluntary process that is conducted by a third-party agency. Such agencies include in their standards a requirement for the independence of governing boards. Independent governance is recognized by national accrediting agencies as closely linked to educational quality. Limit the content, limit the learning. A curriculum based on a particular ideology is more about indoctrination than learning, and that is not the American way. Recent examples of boards appearing to bend to external political pressure have provoked warnings from accreditors. Diversity of thought is a hallmark of American higher education and must not be sacrificed on the altar of partisan politics by board members who are fiduciaries, not thought police.

I was interested in acting on the behalf of students because I myself had worked through a bachelor's degree, a master's degree, and a doctorate degree and therefore knew the classroom from the "other side." Running for the Board of Regents in a five-county district was not daunting to me: I had done my homework; I had run a campaign earlier; I knew the district, and I had spent the intervening years training other women how to be effective candidates.

In the nonpartisan June 1988 primary election, I would run against three opponents, all Republicans. All the counties in the district registered solidly Republican, but I had run against the political odds before and knew they need not be the final decider. Winning over five counties, however, did require participation in a lot more parades, candidate nights, and pancake breakfasts than winning over just one. Door knocking (or precinct walking, as it is known) was where political strategy became important. Identifying dense neighborhoods for coverage efficiency and neighborhoods with a record of high voter turnout was key to the fundamental campaign principle of making candidate time—*my time*—most productive. In rural districts with low population density, hosting and attending community events were crucial. Of course, there were the big ranch dogs to contend with too.

With the help of friends and members of the local Democratic Party chapter, we launched a campaign with an announcement event that drew publicity and good feelings about being together again. I was more comfortable with parades this time around, knowing that an interesting vehicle draws attention and tossing out candy is a big hit. I spent most of my time on doorsteps explaining what a regent does because it is a down-ballot race, placed below that of national and statewide candidates. Once again, those hundreds of conversations I had with constituents would help me learn directly and in detail what people knew and cared about in terms of Nevada's colleges and universities. Polling replaces this individualized activity in high-level races, collapsing multiple views into a few statistics. Talking directly with voters, however, provides personal anecdotes and nuances that deepen an understanding of how their lives are affected by education and government policies. Current races that focus and rely on social media miss rich and irreplaceable opportunities to connect personally with people.

I won the June primary by comfortable margin. John Hawkins, my opponent in the general election, had served as the superintendent of schools in Carson City, the largest city and county in the district. He was widely popular, and we had a friendly relationship, meeting up at candidate events for the next five months. With the help of my campaign team and supporters, I kept knocking on doors. My opponent relied on promotion by mail, special events, and newspaper ads. I did those things too, but walking in his county of residence, where I was less known and he was popular, made a difference. Reflecting later, I realized men might resist knocking on doors, knowing that people—women at home in particular—might not feel comfortable opening their homes to a male stranger. Being a woman, in this case, gave me a direct advantage. Besides, going door-to-door was the part of campaigning I liked best.

In November 1988, I again won comfortably and was sworn in to the Nevada Board of Regents for my first six-year term in January 1989.

I had no idea of what I had signed up for and was in for a surprisingly bumpy start. The official job description of a regent, as called for in the Nevada Constitution and defined by the governing documents of the University of Nevada System (since named the Nevada System of Higher Education, or NSHE), is to carry responsibility for

policy, budgets, hiring the presidents and chancellor, and monitor-
ing their performance. In my first role in political office, I was ready
to take all that on, but what I didn't expect was the near-immediate
initiation into internal politics.

I have always been one to make friends easily. I like people and
am interested in others, an asset in any new setting. Having just completed several years of interviews of Nevadan ranching families for
my dissertation, I was skilled in listening, learning, and taking stock
of unfamiliar situations and dynamics. As a PhD student, I learned
to look for patterns both obvious and beneath the surface, but as a
novice regent, I was immediately put off balance. In my first year, I
felt like I was in a foreign country not knowing the language.

Integrating into any established group requires figuring out who's
who and what's what. In elective office, however, alliances around
particular agendas are what count. I expected transparency and for
my peers to be forthright. The truth was an undercurrent of unspoken agendas ran through and beyond my ability to understand. None
of the norms I knew applied; the domain of politics is less one of
amiable sociability, and more one of competing agendas, strategy,
and interpersonal maneuvering. During my first year on the board,
I chose to observe and listen as much as possible to discern the character and temperament of my new colleagues, and to decipher the
web of unspoken alliances that previous battles had congealed. In
regent meetings, watching policy debates unfold—and participating
in them—over time I was able to sort out the personalities and priorities of my peers.

What I didn't know and learned later was that a few of my new
colleagues and system staff did not see me as neutral, but as an
unknown player who had a reputation as a political activist who
was likely to stir up trouble. I discovered that narrative toward the
end of my first year when the board chair appointed me to lead a
task force looking into a controversy surrounding community college faculty and their unionization efforts. The chancellor's office
and the board viewed these activities with alarm. They were seen,
at least in part, as a response to the faculty's dissatisfaction with the
secondary status of community colleges in a system dominated by
the interests and priorities of Nevada's two universities.

June Whitley, the board's chair, appointed me to head this effort because I was one of two regents representing rural Nevada, where two of Nevada's four community colleges are located. Whitley knew I would bring a fresh and unprejudiced view to the matter. She also knew I had taught anthropology courses at Western Nevada College in Carson City as adjunct faculty and was familiar with the community college landscape firsthand.

One disadvantage that community colleges had long faced in Nevada was that most regents elected to Nevada's governing board were university graduates, and often alumni of one of the two Nevada universities. Few of those elected to govern the community colleges understood the multiple missions these institutions carried out or their important role in workforce training. In recent years, the effort of former presidents of Nevada's community colleges and other advocates to decouple the colleges into a separate governing system reflects that the perception of a tilted playing field persists decades later.

The first step I sought, in 1989, as leader of the Community College Faculty Relations Task Force, was to hold hearings on each community college campus and invite faculty members to testify about their issues and discontent. My proposal was met with stiff resistance by some regents and the chancellor's office staff, who were tasked with organizing these campus efforts. They felt it was a risky approach leading to an uncertain outcome.

"Are predetermined outcomes the requirement around here?" I wondered.

I took it as a given that the outcome of any given query is unknown, or why hold hearings and ask for feedback from those agitating for change? I was dismayed by the uncooperative system staff thwarting my efforts. These "deep state" challenges, as I suppose they are called in national politics, were the first blow to my naivete. I spent much of my first year as a novice regent learning how to navigate on a board where staff played a commanding role and where having allies made a huge difference.

Determined to hold hearings despite the resistance, I confided my frustration to a sympathetic party who was an insider to board rumblings with an ear to the ground. "Nobody's talking to me," I said. "What's going on?" It was in this confidential exchange that I learned a veteran board member known as "the Queen Bee" had started a whisper campaign regarding my supposed activist instincts to stir up trouble. It was said that I was sure to be overly sympathetic to faculty concerns, and so others (including our staff) should not cooperate.

Tension between college and university boards and faculty often goes with the territory. Faculty are in the classroom and in the trenches, whereas boards work from the 30,000-foot level of policy, oversight, fiscal sustainability, and public relations. Because teaching is at the heart of higher education and because I had served as adjunct faculty, I did have a sympathetic ear for faculty concerns. But I was also aware that governance decisions must take all stakeholders into account and look to the long view. I felt I was the right board member to lead the effort to address faculty issues and to possibly head off a widespread unionization attempt if it would be detrimental to the system's well-being.

Facing the resistance challenge, I saw a learning opportunity. I decided to undertake a weeks-long process of holding one-on-one conversations with my fellow regents. I spent several days in Las Vegas, hoping to sit down with each of my colleagues to express my thoughts on the task force and ask theirs. I saw these meetings as a chance to give my peers a firsthand sense of me. This was my best chance to gain a fair hearing—by engaging in face-to-face dialogue.

One regent in particular shared with me the rumor of the "troublemaking Regent Derby" misperception that had been sown and was pleased with my outreach efforts to dispel the myth.

"The rumor doesn't land," he told me, after our conversation.

And still, another regent would not answer my calls.

"She won't meet with me," I confided to UNLV's president, who had a great relationship with all the Las Vegas regents.

"Jill," he said. "Insist!"

I was flummoxed.

"How do you *insist* that somebody meet and talk with you?"

"You tell her you're not leaving town until she agrees to meet with you."

I did as he suggested. The final holdout not only met with me but became an ally, seeing me for who I was rather than the troublemaker I was rumored to be. My public relations campaign paid off and resulted in most of the regents supporting my efforts to move forward with the task force I led. The cooperation of the staff was then assured as well. My first year as a regent confirmed what I already knew about the value of communicating in person, building alliances, and checking my assumptions at the door. It also taught me to press my case and not be intimidated or held back by the rough-and-ready nature of board politics.

For the next several months, the Community College Faculty Relations Task Force conducted listening sessions on each of the four college campuses and then deliberated over what we heard. The faculty were restive and wanted an outcome. The college presidents, who had been anxious over what their faculties might report directly to a regent's committee, were pleased in the end with the attention their institutions received and with our final conclusions.

Following these on-campus sessions and discussions, we determined that our community colleges were not adequately being served under the current structure, which was reflected in faculty discontent. Consequently, we put forth a series of recommendations. Our first was to change the name of the system from the University of Nevada System to the University and Community College System of Nevada (UCCSN). Secondly, we recommended that regent meetings take place on the community college campuses to educate the regents on the critical role community colleges play in educating Nevada's students. We called for the appointment of a vice chancellor for community college affairs and hired one accordingly. (After two years, we discovered that creating such a buffer between the regents and the community colleges was disempowering rather than supportive, and we discontinued the position.)

The reforms enacted because of our monthslong inquiry were a long overdue step in the right direction. The name change was appreciated and symbolically important, but most powerful was the decision to hold regent meetings on the community college campuses. That change involved a major shift in meeting plans, travel, and preparation. The state plane was requisitioned to fly the regents up to Elko for the Great Basin College meetings and more travel was required to periodically get out to Fallon, Western Nevada College's branch campus. The travel and extra burden put on the colleges to host a regents' meeting were well worth the benefit of educating the regents about these colleges. Campus tours were included at these meetings, along with presentations by faculty of institutional highlights and strengths. These presentations particularly exposed the regents to the colleges' important mission, their scope of programs, and the critical role they played in educating Nevadans.

Community colleges provide a crucial pathway to four-year colleges and universities for many of Nevada's posthigh school students. They are often the educational route of choice for Nevada's minority students and are the more affordable option for all students with upwardly mobile aspirations. Community colleges provide a ticket to the middle class, and flexible class scheduling allows community college students to work part- or full-time jobs, which most of them do. The workforce training these colleges provide is a critical engine for Nevada's economic development.

The transfer option for those pursuing a four-year bachelor's degree after completing their first two years at a community college has proven to be not only more affordable but an equal or better educational experience. Research shows that community college students transferring into the universities often perform better than students who begin at the universities. Smaller classes and professors devoted solely to teaching—rather than to teaching, researching, and writing papers to be published—help explain students' educational success. Without the strong and devoted alumni base and glamorous sports programs universities have, community colleges work outside the spotlight, but the impact they have on Nevada's students and economic health is immense. They deserve more support than they have managed to secure in a system where they have always played second fiddle.

The multi-month process of holding hearings and meetings brought more attention to a neglected but critical component of Nevada's higher education system, and the reforms enacted by the board had a statewide impact. The meeting rotation around the state was in effect for decades and was our task force's most consequential outcome. It was not a "predetermined outcome," and it made a lasting difference in Nevada's higher education governance. The reform measures didn't address all the inequities community colleges face in a university-dominated system. For example, the funding gap that prioritizes universities over community colleges was not part of our agenda; it defied efforts before we addressed it and has ever since. Still, our work made a difference, and countless community college faculty thanked me for the role I played in shining the light on the underappreciated jewel of the system that is Nevada's community colleges.

With my first test of leadership chalked up as a success, I felt more confident taking my place on the Board of Regents. I spoke up more in policy debates than I had in my first year and discovered a few allies. Having only viewed higher education from the perspective of a student or faculty member, to be part of the workings behind the screen of governance was nothing short of fascinating.

My next opportunity to take a leadership role and level the playing field on Nevada's campuses came about two years later, when I introduced an initiative to audit the climate for women students and faculty. The phrase "a chilly climate" had emerged in writings about women in the workplace and other organizational settings, and I suspected from my own graduate student experience that women in our Nevada colleges and universities were likely experiencing disadvantages.

Once again, to make a difference, I had to first convince enough of my fellow regents about the appropriateness of the focus. In those first years of my six-year term, we were a board of nine, so convincing at least four other regents was the tipping point to advancing any initiative, policy, or outcome. Getting a few others beyond the four to be at least neutral was important as well, to avoid a block of opposition that could compromise and weaken a robust process of inquiry and advocacy. Four other women were on the board in those early years: Whitley, Carolyn Sparks, Shelley Berkley of Las Vegas, and Dorothy Gallagher of Elko. All but Gallagher supported the initiative. Elko was a conservative county and wrapped in cowboy culture. In conversations with several male colleagues, I found enough backing to push forward. In 1991, a Status of Women Committee was established and because of my lobbying efforts, I was appointed chair.

In determining how to proceed, I once again proposed a campus-by-campus process of inquiry and assessment. And, once again, some of the presidents worried what our findings might disclose and how they might reflect on their leadership. Their concerns were understandable, given that the Board of Regents is the body that holds presidents accountable for their institutions' performance.

To facilitate a campus-by-campus assessment process, I proposed establishing a Status of Women Committee for each institution in the Nevada System of Higher Education. Despite the presidents' concerns, they did not overtly oppose this arrangement. As a result, each campus went about setting up its own Status of Women Committee and determining its leadership. I began quietly hearing how pleased female faculty were with having been given a directive by the regents that granted them the permission and empowerment they needed to address conditions that disadvantaged them in a male-dominated environment.

Make no mistake, males dominated American colleges and universities in the twentieth century. One only need look at the gender profile of college leadership—presidents, vice presidents, and deans—and at professorial salary and advancement differences to get the gender-based imbalance. Beyond the financial and leadership ledger, an equally important area of our focus concerned sexual harassment of female faculty and students. I knew harassment was an issue through accounts shared privately with me while I was a regent. But also in my own graduate student experience, I saw that female peers were vulnerable to the sexual advances of male faculty, who had power over their course grades and career advancement. As in every sector of the economy where men held positions of authority over women, women experienced pressure to comply with overtures and unspoken threats and suggestions from their superiors. It has taken the #MeToo movement of the twenty-first century to finally call out what has been kept in the shadows, yet widely known for decades, about the fate of many women in American institutions and industries.

Worried that our survey results might be diluted if they were passed up through administrative layers at each institution, I spurred the board committee to direct the campus committees to report their findings directly to the regents. The college and university presidents, all men, resisted this unprecedented mandate. Not to imply that maleness alone dictated attitudes about an inquiry into women's experiences on campus, but evidence abounded that men, in their experience as the dominant players, tended to be deaf to women's alternate sense of reality. The twenty-first-century term "mans-plaining" likely comes from a related phenomenon. Thankfully, we regents had final say.

Once the institutions had established their Status of Women Committees, we empowered them to develop campus-specific surveys. The regents offered a model but asked each campus group to tailor it to their particular structure and needs. We requested some content specifics, such as sexual harassment incidence, because we had done our homework reviewing similar efforts at institutions around the country. We wanted specific information about the percentage of female faculty, particularly in science, technology, engineering, and math (STEM) departments, because we knew that their underrepresentation had consequences for female students. Women faculty supported women students, not only as role models, but as mentors as well, in ways that male faculty seldom did. We sought information about the percentage of female students in these STEM programs too.

As chair of the regents' Status of Women Committee, I knew how overarching societal issues limited women's opportunities, but I was eager to learn more specifically about the situation in our colleges and universities. When I heard that Harvard University was offering a three-day course focused on how gender differences in the classroom play out, I jumped at the opportunity and signed up. The course illuminated classroom dynamics that I myself had experienced but never identified.

The leaders of our course at Harvard simulated a classroom experience with the fifty of us—more males than females—in attendance. They facilitated a lengthy question, answer, and discussion session. They then pointed out the dominance of the males, not only in speaking time, or "holding the floor," but also in how their views were repeated and acknowledged by other men in the discussion, when in fact females had made the initial point. The leader pointed out this dynamic of female offerings being repeated but attributed to other male speakers as the discussion continued. Seeing these unequal dynamics in male versus female participation in this staged discussion setting was quite an epiphany and gave me clarity about what I had often witnessed but could not articulate. It was eye-opening to see that my "normal" in discussion was a male-dominated "normal," because it was all I had ever experienced in a classroom.

In my efforts to help level the playing field for future generations of girls and women, I brought what I learned at Harvard back to our deliberations in Nevada.

Our effort on behalf of Nevada's women students and faculty was ahead of its time. A 2020 article written by BYU graduate Brittany Karford Rogers for *Y Magazine* zeroes in on the continuing persistence of female disadvantage in the collegiate mixed-gender classroom. In "When Women Don't Speak," Rogers reports on what BYU researchers Christopher F. Karpowitz, Jessica R. Preece, and Olga Stoddard discovered when looking at what happens when women—who are just as qualified as their male counterparts—are outnumbered: "Having a seat at the table does not mean having a voice," Rogers wrote.

The researchers report that inclusion alone does not level the playing field for women and unless women are the overwhelming majority, they speak less and are interrupted more often. Systematically and across fields, professions, and work/classroom environments, women are viewed as less authoritative than men and their perspectives are taken less seriously. The study offers the startling conclusion that unless the proportion of females to males is four-to-one, women will not have equal time in group discussions. That message echoed what I learned at Harvard decades before. Progress is slow.

After our seven Nevadan institutions completed their surveys, they summarized their findings and presented their reports directly to us, the regents' Status of Women Committee. We wanted to see unfiltered results, and we did. We suspected these assessment efforts would reflect negatively on the institutions, and they did.

The anonymous surveys the campuses conducted disclosed a serious problem with sexual harassment among women faculty. The data on percentages of women faculty and female students in the STEM disciplines were deeply concerning. We learned that a considerable number of female students who began in engineering, for example, dropped out. Lack of female faculty meant less mentoring and support for women students. It also meant less ability to engage in classes, where male students overwhelmingly dominated discussions. Few women in engineering classes resulted in few graduates and even fewer women with doctorates eligible to fill engineering faculty slots. At least that was the rationale given for the imbalance.

We addressed this in our committee recommendations with calls to educate male faculty about supporting and mentoring women students, and to vigorously pursue gender balance in the faculty. Looking back from this twenty-first-century vantage point, progress has been made, but gender imbalance in the STEM disciplines remains an ongoing challenge. I'm pleased we called it out it out in our 1993 Status of Women report.

In terms of our findings on sexual harassment, we recommended and made changes in the University and Community College System of Nevada (UCCSN) Code and Handbook. We called for the separation of parties in sexual harassment claims and time limits to speed up the process of resolving claims. We mandated sexual harassment training on all campuses and convened one for the board itself. Looking back from the current #MeToo movement, which finally grasps what women in male-dominated environments have faced for centuries, our steps seem modest. Yet in 1993, simply calling out sexual harassment as a serious issue that affected women at all levels, systemwide, was a giant first step leading toward reform.

One of the recommendations that came out of our report was that the Status of Women Committees established on each campus were to continue making yearly inquiries and reporting their findings to the regents' committee to ensure continuous oversight and improvement. This practice continued for decades. Eventually, the Status of Women Committee morphed into the Campus Environment Committee and widened its scope to include campus safety and a broader view of diversity and inclusion.

It was satisfying to me, less than halfway into my term, to champion women's equality in Nevada's colleges and universities, particularly considering the work I had done advocating for the Equal Rights Amendment. Regents Berkley, Sparks, and Dan Klaich were key to the success of the Status of Women Committees. Working with them, I quickly learned that allies were essential to getting things done politically.

Klaich, with his family of daughters, was to prove a critical player in another uphill breakthrough battle for women on another regents' committee I chaired—the UNLV Presidential Search Committee. We would lead the search for, and usher in, the first female university president in Nevada, Carol Harter. But first, we had to contend with the contentious high-profile athletics situation at hand.

UNLV basketball, the pride of the Las Vegas sports community, was led by legendary coach Jerry Tarkanian. From his first season as coach in 1973, Tarkanian had built the program from minor rank eventually to its first undefeated season and to a nationally prominent status. By 1992 and the time of his forced retirement, he had led the Runnin' Rebels to the Final Four NCAA championships four times, beating Duke by a NCAA final game record of thirty points in the 1990 national championship. Often affectionately called "Tark the Shark" and known for chewing on a towel on the sidelines during games, Tarkanian was a celebrity. He recruited economically disadvantaged players from junior colleges and was among the first university coaches to have a majority-Black starting lineup.

The attention he garnered, however, was not all positive. The NCAA accused Tarkanian of rule violations and fined him accordingly three times. He battled these accusations, suing the NCAA and winning a settlement of $2.5 million. The president of UNLV at the time, Bob Maxson, was no fan of Tarkanian. Maxson felt the NCAA rule violations were a black eye for the university's academic standing, which he was working to advance. The president, having the power to fire the basketball coach, let it be known it was his intention to do so. The firestorm reaction of the community, for whom Tarkanian was an idol and icon, put the Board of Regents in the crosshairs of a red-hot controversy.

Pressure built between the president's office and the local press that was largely in support of Vegas's beloved coach. All other regent decisions fell by the wayside while this tension escalated. I was still early in my term when this matter rose to the forefront.

Las Vegas, where most Nevada citizens reside, has its own globally distinct reputation, culture, and zeitgeist. Politics in Las Vegas differ from the rest of the state, which lacks the glitz and glitter. As someone perceived by some as a "country girl" from the rural north, I still held a key vote and voice on the Tarkanian issue. It kept me up at night. I wanted to see a middle-ground resolution to a highly emotional battle between two entrenched sides in which compromise seemed impossible.

At a regents' meeting in March 1992, enraged fans stormed the speakers' podium chanting, "How dare you?" and, "We'll get you for this!" Sportswriter Steve Carp called the event "a circus" and Regent Lonnie Hammargren submitted a proposal to hold a sixty-day review of the matter to cool the embers and bring some substance to the dueling positions. President Maxson opposed an extension of time, and a heated debate ensued.

I chose to support the proposal as a "cooling off," to avoid the clear disregard of vociferous community outcry on the one hand, or rejection of presidential prerogative on the other. I smiled when I read Carp's characterization of my comments: "Jill Derby, the Queen of Gardnerville, deserved special kudos for her caring and willingness to address the issue fairly from both sides."

My side lost that vote, clearing the way for Maxson's course of terminating Tarkanian's contract. There was to be no deference to community passions. Some of us, behind the scenes, urged the president to allow the popular coach a hero's exit, but he, having won the battle, chose otherwise. That choice may have been a factor in his loss of support from enough regents over the ensuing year to end what could have been a far longer presidency at UNLV.

Winning a split vote is rarely an unequivocal victory. Those on the losing side of a close vote don't always acquiesce with grace, particularly when strong feelings are involved and when the public who elected them to office is not happy with their choice. Following the Tarkanian vote, recall efforts were initiated against Regents Joe Foley and Sparks, both strong supporters of Maxson. Given that my district was four hundred miles north of Las Vegas and far removed from the passions of UNLV sports, I had immunity to any angry backlash from the community, and anyway, I had voted to respect their concerns.

It would be hard to underestimate the enormity of civic pride Las Vegans felt in the success of their university basketball team. Only in recent decades had the city been elevated from a dusty desert town to the glittering symbol of fun and fortune that draws tourists from around the world. UNLV, less than thirty years old and known as "Tumbleweed Tech" in earlier decades, was now the proud home of the Runnin' Rebels. Sending their beloved coach packing was not something Las Vegans would quickly forget.

The 1992 dustup between the community and the campus

wouldn't be the last time my vote was cast in a critical UNLV stand-off. In 1995, I would once again find myself facing a split board vote, but this time, to my great relief and enduring pride, I ended up on the majority side. Leading the UNLV Presidential Search Committee that resulted in the hiring of Nevada's first woman university president involved a search process that took the better part of a year and ended with me in the hospital with a heart episode.

In 1994, as President Maxson stepped down, the embers still glowed from the bitter feud between the city's diehard basketball fans and its university regents. The recall efforts of the two Las Vegas regents had proved unsuccessful; tensions between the town and gown, or the community and the regents, remained fraught. The task of hiring a new university president lay before the board, and it was clear that the atmosphere surrounding the search would be tense. The process and outcome were going to be closely watched by all with a stake in UNLV's future.

The board selected Kenny Guinn as interim UNLV president during the yearlong selection process that was to follow. Guinn had served as superintendent of Clark County schools from 1969 to 1978. Moving out of the realm of education, he served for nine years as vice president and then president of Nevada Savings and Loan. In 1987, he stepped down from his bank position to serve as chief executive officer and board chair of the Southwest Gas Corporation. He was widely known, liked, and highly regarded in the Las Vegas community, and thus seen by the regents as a safe choice to temporarily lead the university.

Being tapped as the regent to head the critical search for the next UNLV president surprised me. On the surface, I seemed an unlikely choice to lead this key task in Nevada's biggest and most politically prominent city. Although I was an alumna of UNLV, I was a newer regent and a woman from a rural county far from Vegas. Few Las Vegans knew of Carson Valley or where it was located. In retrospect, board chair Jim Eardley likely hoped to buffer the anticipated political pressures by appointing a regent whose re-election would not depend on support from the Las Vegas community. I was up for re-election the following year, but few in my district had any stake in the UNLV presidential search. Without a dog in the fight, I seemed a safe choice. My supposed immunity did not last long.

Nevada, having strict open meeting laws, did not permit high levels of secrecy in university presidential searches. Although a search consultant would be hired to help recruit and vet candidates, the finalist pool, which is where public interest concentrates, would be a highly visible, contentious, and public affair. It was my first experience leading a presidential search. Fortunately, the other regents appointed to the search committee were some of the smartest and most thoughtful to work with—veteran Regents Klaich and Foley, and first-termers Berkley and Dave Phillips.

Members of the UNLV faculty and larger campus community were nervous about the transition ahead. Maxson had been a popular leader. The rift within the larger community over the dismissal of Tarkanian still hung in the air, and faculty worried that the city's passion for athletic success would dominate the process. Prominent Las Vegas voices were weighing in through their elected representatives on the Board of Regents.

Along with the regents' UNLV Presidential Search Committee, our process called for a Campus Advisory Committee made up of faculty, administrative staff, alumni, and community representatives. I prescribed that the two committees meet together to allay faculty concerns about the role politics might play and to build a sense of collegiality and common purpose between the campus group and the regent's committee. In all cases, the Campus Advisory Committee would vote first in its advisory capacity, and the regents' committee would make the final decision.

Determining a profile of what would best serve UNLV's future leadership requirements needed to be done thoroughly and inclusively. We hired a consultant for that purpose and spent the next months convening various campus and community groups and holding one-on-one interviews with key stakeholders. What became clear in the resulting report was that the faculty and campus constituencies wanted an academic leader first and foremost. Community voices varied, but there was clear interest also in building on Tarkanian's legacy of nationally prominent athletic programs. Alumni everywhere take pride in high-profile sports teams that allow them to cheer on their alma mater and bask in national recognition. Indeed, academics versus athletics is a familiar point of contention in the academic world.

Transparency was critical, and we chose to conduct an open search, with the finalist pool of candidates known to the campus and community. The topic of open versus closed executive searches is a controversial one in higher education circles: traditional wisdom holds that strong candidates won't apply for fear of not being selected. Such transparency can dissuade sitting presidents, who do not want to take the risk of public exposure, from applying. Presidential searches therefore tend to attract those in the ranks of rising talent, at the vice president and provost levels of university administration. Counter to that argument is the case that being a finalist in a major university presidential search is a credit in one's career if one has not already been a president or is a president of a lesser institution.

No matter what, transparency has its own rewards: it garners trust, particularly among the faculty, and it dispels conspiracy theories about deals struck in the hallways by a handful of regents with their own contacts and insider agendas. New presidents who are selected with the input of campus constituencies tend to have a smoother transition stepping into their leadership role than presidents whose appointments are decided by a board without campus input. When faculties oppose a particular appointment, presidents are likely to find a lack of support in establishing their authority, and they may find their tenure negatively affected.

Colleges and universities are not like corporations with their strict hierarchical authority structure. Presidents have to navigate between the "shared governance" expectations of faculty, who are at the heart of the academic enterprise, and the governance authority of their boards. This is not always an easy channel to pilot.

The executive search firm we hired conducted a national search, and both committees reviewed the files of applicants. It was a long and arduous process. We used the leadership profile that had been developed over months of consultation with all stakeholders to guide the winnowing process and ultimately arrived at a small pool of finalists. Coincidentally, included in this pool were two sitting presidents: a woman with strong academic credentials from an institution with only Division 3 athletic programs, and a man from a midwestern university with dominant Division 1 athletic teams. These finalists were chosen through meetings and votes of both the Campus Advisory Committee and the regents' panel of five.

The next step involved inviting the finalists to Las Vegas for interviews and two-day campus visits that involved a presentation to the faculty and campus groups as well as meetings with other stakeholders. These went smoothly. Also included were evening events with two or three regents who were not on the search committee. These did not go smoothly. Instead, these evening events, meant to engender informal, get-to-know-you conversations, ended up being discordant occasions where various individuals attempted to influence the outcome of the search process by dissuading one candidate from continuing the process. One regent, in fact, flew to Las Vegas to deliver her message in person—a message suggesting that UNLV was not ready for a woman president. When I learned this, I was livid. I am a strong believer that a fair and open process is critical to a fair and open result, and subversion must not influence an outcome.

Immediately, I sprang into action: the female finalist and I huddled, with me encouraging her to stay the course, saying, "We aren't going to allow a small group of good ol' boys and their allies to decide this outcome, are we!"

She rallied to the message. I then alerted my fellow search committee regents to what was transpiring and had a tough confrontation with one of the instigators, who apologized, claiming that his insulting comments to the candidate resulted from one too many drinks. He sent flowers to her hotel room as a peace offering. After five years on the board, I was seasoned enough to know that playing nice was not what was called for in keeping the search on track and credible to the UNLV campus community, whose leadership we were determining.

It is not unheard of that university presidential searches are subverted by greased-in candidates with strong ties to particular board members, disrespectful of campus consultation and sentiment. I was a strong advocate of the organizational wisdom, "Good processes result in good outcomes," and that wide support for a final decision results from processes that are consultative and transparent. People appreciate being consulted in the decisions that affect their working lives, and they cooperate more when their voices are heard and respected. Our process did result in a good outcome, but it was a rutted road getting there, right up to the regents' meeting where the search committee presented its recommendation of Carol Harter to be the next UNLV president.

The half-hour debate that followed our recommendation was the tensest and most heated I can recall. The four regents who supported the candidate with the stronger background in athletic programs were not about to concede defeat, having told their favored candidate (I learned later) that he had the job in the bag. With the five of us on the Presidential Search Committee firmly committed to our recommended candidate, the remaining two regents (we were a board of eleven by that time) were caught in the middle of an increasingly heated deliberation. Back and forth it went. One of the two undecided regents eventually signaled his alignment with the opposition to the committee's recommendation. That left the eleventh regent, still undecided, as the swing and deciding vote. The suspense was palpable. My heart was beating overtime. A year's effort, with so much at stake, and it all came down to one regent, one vote.

She swung our way, and Harter was elected UNLV's next president. I was flooded with relief and joy.

Leaving the building soon after celebrating, I would have a short conversation that brought me to tears. I was riding down in the elevator from the third floor to the lobby with a maintenance woman. "I just heard," she said. "They elected a woman to be our next president. I can't believe it. I'm so happy!"

I started to respond, but my voice cracked. Tears filled my eyes. I knew that this woman's sense of pride was resonating in women's conversations across the UNLV campus and beyond. UNLV did it! Nevada had its first female university president.

I flew home to Gardnerville filled with satisfaction of a job well done and looking forward to decompressing and resuming a more normal pace. Our next regent meeting was blessedly two months away. I couldn't have anticipated what transpired the next day.

I was running a simple errand at the town pharmacy when I noticed an odd feeling in my chest, like my heart was not beating normally. I had never paid attention to my heart before, but something felt off, strange. Coincidentally, an emergency medical center was across the way, so I walked over and told the woman at the reception station that my heart was behaving strangely. In seconds, she was around the desk leading me by the arm through swinging doors, summoning help, and helping me onto a gurney. Her sense of urgency alarmed me. I hadn't thought much was wrong, but her sense of haste left me uncertain. The emergency staff quickly hooked me up to a heart monitor, and I could hear the thump, thump, skip-a-beat thump. I had given them Steve's number when they asked whom they could call, still not sure this was a matter of such heightened emergency.

What happened next changed my perception dramatically: The heart monitor at my side, which had been sounding the irregular thumping of my heart, suddenly stopped. In total shock, I assumed my heart had stopped and I was dying. I toppled over and passed out cold.

The next thing I knew, I was being shaken awake.

"What happened?" they asked.

Trying to clear my head, I told them, "My heart stopped!"

"No," they said. "Your heart didn't stop. What made you think so?"

"I heard it stop on the monitor. It stopped."

Eyes rolled in relief: someone had simply muted the machine.

"I wish you had told me," I said.

Feeling a bit foolish but shaken by the experience of having my life flash before my eyes, I was worse for wear. I had been in much better condition walking through the emergency clinic doors. Now, they were telling me, moral support was on its way. Steve had been out at John Ascuaga's ranch pregnancy-testing cattle. With no phone access (pre-cell phone era), an assistant from his veterinary hospital had to race out to the ranch and into the field to deliver the alarming message of where I had landed myself. It took Steve fifteen minutes more to drive to where I was still hooked up to the silent heart monitor, awaiting an ambulance to take me to the hospital. I was terribly relieved when he rushed in, pale-faced over the word he had received of my whereabouts. Reassuring him that I would be okay, I was loaded into an ambulance.

I spent that night in the Carson Tahoe Hospital under the care of a cardiologist who decided that my irregular heartbeat was probably stress-related and not a cause for major concern or intervention. Back home, my heart settled back into its regular rhythm, and

I hoped the brouhaha over the close vote of the board would fade quickly and life as a regent could return to normal.

In the months that followed, I was soon again engaged in an election campaign to defend my seat on the board. I was seeking a second term and had a serious opponent in Mark Amodei, an attorney in Carson City, another Republican stronghold. Still, I knew the district well, campaigned hard, and won my second term with only one heart-stopping moment: the night of the election, we miscomputed the voting totals coming in from five different counties and thought my opponent had won. When I called Amodei to concede, he said my concession might be premature, but I didn't think so. I called my closest regent colleague and friend Shelley Berkley and said, "I lost." She told me later that she went right to bed and pulled the covers over her head, not willing to face life without me on the board.

Early the next morning, to my great astonishment and relief, my victory was announced—it turned out I had won handily. Amodei never called me back to concede, violating election convention and etiquette, but my dear friend Shelley slept better that night and so did I.

In 1995, when Harter assumed the presidency of UNLV, I had just been elected board vice chair, and as such had the pleasure of performing the investiture at the October inauguration ceremony. I was not disappointed when board chair, Maddy Graves, who had not supported her appointment, was unavailable that day.

Because of the split decision of the eleven-member board and the lingering hostility of board members who supported the alternate candidate, the first year of Harter's presidency was rocky. Best practice for governing boards instructs that when you lose a vote, you go quietly into the night and support the majority choice of your fellow board members. Regents, however, do not always follow the rules, particularly when strong passions are involved. Shifting alignments and opportunities to contrarian positions followed. In the end, the strong fundraising results that President Harter demonstrated, even in her first year, were the closing argument that the board had chosen well.

Harter's eleven-year tenure as UNLV's first woman president resulted in major advances for the university. Following her departure, a building was named after her to recognize her contributions to UNLV's growth in enrollment and academic stature. Among her many impressive accomplishments, she added sixty masters and doctoral programs and raised more than $550 million in private gifts and pledges (a figure that represented 77 percent of the funds that had been raised over the course of the twenty-five prior years). She created Nevada's first law school and first dental school, and she was the founding executive director of the Beverly Rogers, Carol C. Harter Black Mountain Institute: International Center for Creative Writing and Scholars.

There were many more successes to President Harter's credit, and importantly, she was well liked by UNLV faculty and students. I was grateful that we had persisted through the sometimes-bruising experience of breaking a glass ceiling, and I put all the lessons learned into my toolkit of strategies for battles yet to come.

Nevada might not have a Nevada State College (NSC) if a couple of us hadn't put our full weight of advocacy behind it. A group of Henderson leaders first proposed the idea, and it became "a hill to die on" for me in those last years of the twentieth century.

In 1997, my first year as board chair and with the leadership of Chancellor Richard Jarvis and Vice Chancellor Jane Nichols, the board launched an initiative to create a master plan for the entire system of higher education. It was a big undertaking, and I was an enthusiastic supporter, agreeing with the adage, "If you don't know where you're going, any road will get you there."

To kick off our effort, we brought in the RAND Corporation to help us look decades ahead into the twenty-first century and plan for the higher education needs of Nevada. Its findings, partly based on Nevada's rapid growth trajectory, predicted a fast-growing need for teachers, nurses, and other professions requiring a baccalaureate degree level of education. With the universities' growing focus on advanced degrees and research, RAND recommended the creation of a higher education middle category—one that fell between the community colleges and universities—a state college tier of institutions. Its data and projections were compelling: almost all larger states had state colleges, and Nevada, with its ballooning population, was becoming more like Arizona and less like Wyoming. I was all in on the plan, excited by the expanded access a state college would provide Nevada's students. Henderson was the designated site.

Not everyone was enthusiastic. Colleges and universities find themselves in competition for student enrollment, and they don't often welcome a new competitor. Many southern regents, feeling allegiance to UNLV or College of Southern Nevada (CSN), did not signal support for the initiative. The early resistance established opposing sides.

Nichols, in a letter of recommendation in support of a National Trustee Award for which I was nominated in 2005, referred to my "iron will." I never saw myself in that light but suspect she was referring particularly to the determination I brought the Nevada State College initiative. I had a strong ally too, in Regent Thalia Dondero, who stepped in as board chair after me in 2000.

Having the recommendation of the RAND Corporation on our side was critical. We lobbied hard with our fellow regents and finally overcame the dissent with a majority vote. Nevada State College was established in 2002. When you want to advance any huge initiative, I learned it is best to commission a study to recommend it.

The first president selected to lead Nevada State College (NSC) was Richard Moore, who had been the popular and successful president of CSN in Las Vegas. Committed to identifying the best practices of recently established colleges, he arranged for a group of us to travel with him to visit the West's newest colleges and universities, including The Evergreen State College in Washington, Portland State College in Oregon, and the new California State Universities of San Marcos and Monterey Bay. It was interesting and instructive to hear about the challenges brand-new colleges face and a few of the frantic make-do solutions required when they open their doors for the first time.

President Moore got NSC off to a good start, and I was happy and proud to be at its dedication. I was even prouder, after stepping off the board, that my daughter, Tobyn Derby-Talbot, already holding a baccalaureate degree, was a graduate in NSC's first class of nursing. The college has persisted and thrived despite budget challenges that require it to compete for funding with UNLV and UNR (which has never been a level playing field). It is my hope, envisioned in the

RAND study, that more than one state college will be commissioned to serve Nevada's growing student population.

Another highlight of my third and final term on the Board of Regents (2000–2006) came amid both the challenges of our growing higher education system and board dynamics that required time and attention as new regents came on board. The Desert Research Institute (DRI) is one of NSHE's jewels, but it often gets less notice than the colleges and universities with their students, athletic teams, and alumni. DRI, which focuses on environmental research, was incorporated into NSHE in 1969, after a ten-year initial placement under the umbrella of UNR.

Its early mission had a Nevada focus, relating to the management and understanding of our state's arid land resources, establishing a cloud-seeding project to enhance water supply in the state's north, and studying groundwater in the southern regions where atomic testing took place. As DRI grew, it expanded its research focus and faculty to address environmental issues on a global scale, and in time developed cutting-edge research projects on every continent. In the years of its existence, the institute and its distinguished faculty have achieved worldwide renown.

One of DRI's most noted global collaborations involved two of its air quality experts, Judith Chow and John Watson. Chow and Watson collaborated with Chinese researchers in efforts to preserve the ancient Terra Cotta Warriors, circa 221 BCE, discovered in Xi'an, China, in 1974. The exposure of the statues to air pollution following their excavation was causing rapid deterioration, and much of the pollution was caused by almost two million tourists visiting the enclosed museum annually. DRI's president at the time, Stephen Wells, signed a memorandum of understanding with the Chinese Academy of Science Institute to devise solutions to address air quality issues and propose remediation. More than eight thousand more warriors, horses, and chariots remained underground, and further excavation was delayed until preservation efforts could be developed to protect them.

In 2005, during my repeat term as the board's vice chair, Wells and a small delegation from DRI, including scientists Chow and Watson, were heading to Xi'an to meet with their Chinese counterparts and a high-level delegation from the Chinese Cultural Ministry and the Chinese Academy of Sciences. They were to formalize the agreement and celebrate their collaboration over this unique and celebrated archaeological site. Wells, sensitive to Chinese cultural perceptions, felt a need to include a comparable "high-level" government representative to accompany and balance the American delegation, reinforcing official support for the project to match to the Chinese delegation's official representatives. Given the Board of Regents' governing authority in Nevada, he invited then board chair Stavros Anthony to accompany the delegation for the five-day trip. To my good fortune, Anthony declined the offer because of scheduling conflicts and Wells turned to me. I leapt at the chance.

As an anthropologist, I had followed the remarkable story of the local farmer who had discovered the ancient terra cotta figures while digging in his field.

We flew to Beijing and then to Xi'an, where the Chinese regally treated us with ceremonial and special events. A dinner and theatrical performance stand out in my memory. Best of all was our visit to the enclosed site of the excavated warriors, which was closed to other visitors during our excursion. We were allowed to go down to the ground level, an area cordoned off to tourists, to admire the warriors close up and take photos. I was thrilled to stand beside these perfectly preserved 2,200-year-old relics of Chinese imperial history, created to guard Emperor Qin She Huang's tomb. Like all the ancient sites I have visited, it put America's short history in perspective.

I flew back separately, while the rest of the delegation stayed for more meetings and activities. On a three-day stopover in Beijing, I visited the Great Wall, a day's excursion from the city. It was all I had imagined it would be. It was a cold, windy day in early March, but bundled in my wool coat I hiked along the wall for several hours, marveling at its ancient construction and the history it told. Back in Beijing, I visited the Palace Museum, the Forbidden City, and the Summer Palace. I rode around in a bicycled *tuk-tuk* in one of the fast-disappearing ancient Hutong neighborhoods with its narrow alleys and simple traditional houses behind high walls. Lucky for me, I even got a glimpse of the gardened dwellings behind the walls because my guide had a friend who invited us in and served us tea.

Almost all those neighborhoods I enjoyed visiting have since been converted to modern construction and skyscrapers in China's fast-paced urban renewal efforts.

During my years of traveling the world following college, while living and working in the Middle East, I had many opportunities to visit the sites of ancient civilizations in the Mediterranean, Egypt, and Mesopotamia. These were often profound experiences for me, as were my excursions in China, and even my hikes up to the ancient Bristlecone Pine trees in Nevada's Great Basin Park. Such ancient wonders shrink one's sense of being in time in comparison to the grand sweep of millennia that comprise human history. These are humbling ego-checking experiences, and they are always also educational.

Back home in Nevada, at our next regents' meeting, President Wells reported on the DRI-China collaboration and our visit to Xi'an. Not surprisingly, Regent Steve Sisolak, in a potential "gotcha" moment, asked who had paid my expenses. Having anticipated the question, I was happy to answer simply, "I did."

Those 2005 regent meetings were often tense affairs. The board had appointed Las Vegas luminary, Jim Rogers, NSHE chancellor in 2004, and the years that followed were as turbulent as any during my long tenure on the board. In the early nineties, when a group of us set in motion a transition to a "stronger" chancellor model, we had no vision of what that might evolve into in the decades ahead. We especially had no idea how everyone would fare in the hands of a wealthy media mogul with a volatile temperament and no experience in higher education governance. We would soon find out.

CHAPTER 5

The Chancellor Chronicles

Fraught is too strong a term to characterize the history of the Nevada System of Higher Education (NSHE) chancellor–Board of Regents relationship, but smooth and harmonious miss the mark as well. When trust, good communication, and a sense of common purpose prevail, the dynamic is good news for NSHE, but different personalities bring different expectations to their roles and conflict can develop. Two lanes of authority, one for the chancellor and another for the board, is the ideal, but boundary lines can blur in actual practice, and relations can fray if board members become critical of the chancellor's leadership or leadership style. With thirteen bosses (the number of regents had grown from eleven at that time), it can be hard to please everyone. In my eighteen-year tenure on the board, we cycled through four chancellors and in no case was the pressure for change unanimous.

A critical link in state systems of higher education such as exist in Nevada is the position of the system head, called the "chancellor" in our state. The regents select a chancellor to represent their authority over the institutions that comprise the system—the two universities, four community colleges, one state college, and the Desert Research Institute. One of the ongoing tensions that characterize such a system of colleges and universities is the tug of war between centralized power and authority (the chancellor and board) and decentralized authority (the individual colleges and universities).

My tenure on the Nevada Board of Regents was bookended by a swing from decentralized toward centralized, and a model of weak chancellor to strong. The fifteen-year arc of that swing was away from a loosely decentralized system, which left the individual institutions free from top-down direction and accountability, to stronger central control by the regents and the system office headed by the chancellor. The arc was more dramatic than initially intended. It veered from the hands of even-tempered Mark Dawson in the eighties to the storied firebrand, run-the-show Jim Rogers in 2004. Some directives put in motion go further than intended. A group of us on the board in the early nineties initiated that shift. More on the Jim Rogers saga to follow.

A second tension that repeatedly arises in Nevada, which has recently erupted in a rancorous public display, is the push and pull between the board and the chancellor. The regents hire a chancellor to be the chief administrative officer over the system, but retain their ultimate authority, prescribed in the state constitution. Chancellors see themselves as empowered to manage the system of colleges and universities according to the policy guidelines laid out by the regents. The regents, for their part, are protective of their own final authority over the institutions and can slide into dispute among themselves over which faction's priorities with which the chancellor is aligned. When there is unanimity among the board of thirteen, harmony prevails; but when that unity frays, discord follows, and a chancellor's odds of longevity are unlikely. Having a board of thirteen bosses can be a difficult balancing act for a chancellor, and if support weakens with five or six of the regents, a chancellor's future employment may be in doubt.

During my tenure on the board, and in the years that have followed, a group of regents' disenchantment with the chancellor has been the primary cause of turnover in that office. It has rarely been a smooth transition because of the chancellor's retirement goals or better job opportunities. It is more likely baked into the challenge of a single individual trying to meet the concerns of and answer to a diverse collection of citizens who choose to seek the elective office of Nevada regent. A popular saying in higher education circles comes to mind: "Board governance is a team sport, but most board members are quarterbacks." As experienced coaches know, that can make for an unpredictable field of play.

The tension between centralized and decentralized mirrors that of the federal government and the individual states. Individual states like the inflow of federal money into their coffers but resent direction on how to spend it. The same is true for Nevada's colleges and universities. There are advantages to a system approach to managing the state's higher education institutions; the advantages include funding arrangements and articulation agreements that allow students to matriculate between institutions—particularly from community colleges to universities.

But from the institutions' point of view, there are disadvantages. To begin with, colleges and universities are highly competitive with each other. Each looks out for their own interests and advantages that push up against the system's priorities. When it is president against president and each for themselves, the strongest voices command most of the limited bounty. Being the "strongest," for one thing, means having the most supporters and alumni in the legislature and having longevity to cultivate strong ties. During my tenure, not surprisingly, that advantage fell to the University of Nevada, Reno (UNR), which has been around for more than a hundred years and benefits from the legislature being close to its campus, alumni, and supporters. Regents in the Las Vegas area were well aware of what they considered an unfair advantage of UNR, their primary rival, which may have energized the effort to strengthen the system voice through empowering the chancellor with greater authority.

In 1993, a group of us commissioned a study to consider a different model of system governance that would delegate greater authority to the chancellor as system head. We reasoned that without a strong chancellor invested with some levers of control over the institutions, the Board of Regents' authority was weakened and institutional competition for resources would rule the day. One lever of empowerment for the role was charging the chancellor with the responsibility of evaluating presidential performance. This was viewed as a major change in the system-institutional power balance, but we saw it as the best way a chancellor and the regents could exert authority over the system of competing institutions.

As a follow-up to the study and its recommendations, the board accepted the retirement of the sitting chancellor, who only had a master's degree (all the presidents had doctoral degrees) and who was most comfortable playing the role of coordinator. Those of us who served as the instigators of this transition to stronger centralized authority served on the search committee and wrote the job description of the leader we sought accordingly. We searched and hired Richard Jarvis, who came with a British accent and a PhD in geography from Cambridge University via an associate provost position in the New York State System of Higher Education. We hired him with the goal of empowering the system head with the authority to carry out the regents' priorities, to lead with a system focus, and to referee the competitive playing field among our institutions. We could not have foreseen the unintended consequences this major policy shift would provoke in decades to come. The board was genuinely pleased with the change in leadership and the new sense of system agency that came with it. Jarvis was smart, articulate, and a quick study about what was expected in the office of the chancellor under the new direction the regents' sought. His delightful sense of humor smoothed the transition in leadership, and the new era of stronger system guidance began.

Other pressures called for change. The University of Nevada, Las Vegas (UNLV), and its strongest advocates on the board felt for some time that the deck had been stacked against their university. UNLV was a new kid on the block by comparison (only established in the late fifties) and thus had a smaller alumni base than UNR and less time to grow and establish its footing in the Nevada higher education landscape. Regent Joe Foley was a leading advocate of this view and at meetings railed against the system funding formula, which he felt was rigged in favor of UNLV's northern peer and rival, UNR. Joe Crowley, the long-serving UNR president, defended the fairness of the funding allocation.

Board meetings to approve the system budget, which laid out the funds directed to each institution, were often rancorous, with regents representing Las Vegas vocal about their concerns of UNR fiscal favoritism. State senator Bill Raggio, a Republican from Washoe County, whose power was decisive in the legislature in those years, was an alumnus and strong supporter of UNR. He influenced budgetary outcomes in ways that fed UNLV suspicions of an unequal playing field. That narrative of disadvantage characterized UNLV's posture well into the twenty-first century and was only mitigated by the establishment of the south's own medical school and the increasing dominance of southern legislators, driven by the rapid growth of Las Vegas and the resulting demographic shift in the state. That rivalry between the two universities is ongoing and most on display at the annual face-offs in football and basketball.

The story of the four different chancellors who served during my tenure as regent reflects another theme of potential tension that arose periodically and led to disruptions in the NSHE system leadership. Chancellors serve at the pleasure of the board, and their relationship with individual regents affects their longevity. Of the four chancellors who spanned the decades in which I served, it was largely board divisions and politics that led to the turnover. In every case, when a chancellor lost the support of most of the board—whether the eleven-member board in the nineties, or the thirteen-member board after reapportionment in 2000—his or her fate was sealed.

Chancellor Jarvis, who served six years with high distinction, led the effort to develop a systemwide master plan. But he miscalculated that having the support of the governor and legislative leadership, along with three or four of the strongest, most respected regents, was sufficient. When turnover brought new faces to the boardroom, some of whom were not convinced he equally respected all his bosses, the wheels of transition were set in motion. The addition of several new regents into the mix of the board's interpersonal relations can shift a dynamic that existed before their arrival. Since alliances are critical in voting outcomes, sitting regents are often active in seeking good relations with newly elected ones and drawing their support into their own ways of viewing the system and their areas of interest and focus. As in any elective or appointed body, new members with their priorities and agendas can create a different landscape for a chancellor to navigate.

Following the Jarvis chancellorship, Jane Nichols, vice chancellor for academic affairs, was tapped to fill that slot. Whatever gender challenges women chief executive officers face in every venue (and they are considerable), Nichols was smart, knowledgeable, and so interpersonally gracious that she was well-liked and respected in all quarters. She led the system with distinction for four years.

Effective governance and growth characterized her tenure until a controversial decision by the board brought rancor and division. When the regents voted in 2003 to terminate the popular president of the College of Southern Nevada (CSN) rather than face the resignation of the chancellor in the dispute over who had the final say for the system and its institutions in the legislative budget advocacy, a period of divisiveness and turmoil began. It had been a one-vote margin by the board, and both the political fallout and the interpersonal rupture of board members were intense.

Without a doubt, it was the toughest vote I ever had on the board. There were few times in our high-impact board decision sessions when competing positions had so much at stake. Whichever way the vote went, I knew there would be huge repercussions for the system. Friendships were also at stake. I didn't want to be in that room, faced with that decision, on the fateful day. I wanted to be anywhere else. It was not surprising that the board vote split, 7–6. What was clear to me was a central governance principle: the integrity and authority of NSHE over the individual institutions were on the line. It was that integrity I felt sworn to uphold as a system regent. If individual colleges could end-run NSHE in budget advocacy to the legislature, then the value and rationale for having a statewide system of colleges and universities, led by the board and the chancellor, was seriously undermined. I voted reluctantly with the majority.

In the current legislative climate in Washington, DC, we hear reports that members of opposing parties rarely mingle socially as they did in earlier eras. Partisan feelings and rancor run so deep that enmity has infected the interpersonal terrain of elected representatives, such that they rarely speak to each other personally. Although not driven by a partisan divide, the same dynamic applied to Nevada's regents. The nonpartisan nature of the board held well in my tenure, but controversial issues where passionate positions were held, followed by a close vote, often led to bitter feelings. Previous alliances ruptured, and new ones formed. Who sat next to whom at lunches or dinners was affected. Strong feelings about the rightness of a particular issue (and we are all sure we are right about our opinions) always took time to abate, at least until the next hot issue formed new alliances and rivals.

All representative groups, whether they are civil, religious, or professional, have their internal politics. Without focused efforts by leaders to ensure civility by encouraging person-to-person connection, strong feelings and majority rule can easily fray relationships among competing voices. Like a turn of a kaleidoscope, new configurations emerge. Tough issues are those with solid rational and major constituencies on opposing sides. Having to make weighty decisions that affect lives and cause hostile blowback caused me stress while in office and led others to leave.

In 2004, Chancellor Nichols, who had developed hearing loss

from a health episode, felt it was time to step down after just four years. She may also have been weary from contentiousness on the board. Her invaluable contribution to Nevada higher education continued for many more years in other capacities: she served both as vice chancellor again under her successor, Jim Rogers, and later she worked on the senior administrative team at Truckee Meadows Community College. Nichols typified a leader for whom service to students and their education came ahead of any personal agenda in whatever capacity she served. High-profile churn and clashes, and often public disruptions, marked the next era in the Board of Regents' history.

I didn't know Jim Rogers, but I was aware of his name and reputation, as did anyone who spent time and did business in Las Vegas. He was a controversial local luminary and a media mogul who had entered the fray of Clark County School District board politics. Many knew of his short fuse. There were accounts of Rogers firing employees on a moment's notice for having a messy desk or ordering in food, only to rehire them when his reason returned. That he was difficult to work with was well documented in press accounts, including a 2000 *Las Vegas City Life* cover story that pointed out his incendiary nature. When he threw his hat in the ring to serve as interim chancellor, many wondered why the board even considered his appointment.

Because of his reputation for being difficult and his total lack of higher education experience, I opposed appointing Rogers to be our interim chancellor. I was surprised, however, to learn that I was in the minority. He had the support of all the regents who represented the Las Vegas area. They formed the majority from the start, and that sealed the deal. I was poised to be on the losing side of an upcoming vote on the matter. The calculation I weighed, being on the losing side of that vote, was how I could have the most impact after the fact. By voting against the motion, I could speak publicly of the risk of handing the leadership reins to someone who had no track record in education leadership, and particularly to someone with a history of strong opinions, a volatile temperament, and the megaphone of a media company to advance his own agenda. I thought bringing Rogers in was not only risky, but crazy.

In the end, I voted with the majority, out of the political calculation of how I might best protect the system from what I worried lay ahead. Voting against his nomination might alienate me from someone I hoped to influence—Rogers himself. Howard Rosenberg was the one honest "no" vote. His objections were exactly mine, but I abandoned my conscience, voted pragmatically, and made a different choice. As the elected representatives of the body entrusted with fiduciary and policy responsibility for Nevada's colleges and universities, selecting leadership is among the most consequential decisions the board makes. I feared things would not go well. Early on, they didn't.

Rogers was appointed interim chancellor and had only been in office a few months when he shot off a three-page memo to our board comparing us negatively to the Arizona Board of Regents, which he knew from his association with its law school (the Arizona board is smaller and appointed by the governor). He then laid out a seven bullet-point list of everything that was wrong with our board and NSHE in a derogatory tone. He pointed out that we were too large and unsophisticated to function efficiently. He pointed out "waste" in institutional spending and to our inadequacy in controlling the presidents. He pointed to our own lapses in congeniality and collegiality, in his typical hyperbole, as "hatreds." He claimed that without centralized control, the presidents and faculty would continue to "divide and conquer" the system.

Having come from a business background, Rogers was unfamiliar with the shared governance tradition in higher education, which is collaborative and consultive. His memo made clear that coming from a corporate management model, he was quick to take command in a top-down, authoritative manner and intended to take charge and fix everything. I read over his memo, dated August 31, 2004, and his list of our failings, not surprised, but annoyed: he seemed to cast himself in a savior role and in service to that, overstated what he saw as needing an overhaul. I figured we could use his disparaging assessment and overstated list of concerns as fodder for a useful conversation in our next board meeting—and as a way to forge a constructive working partnership with our new interim chancellor. As I learned to my dismay the next day, a working partnership wasn't what Rogers had in mind. He leaked his memo to the press, essentially publicly trashing the Board of Regents and the system. I was livid.

I only flew to Las Vegas in a fit of pique and high dudgeon twice during my tenure as regent: first, to protect the UNLV presidential search from underhanded efforts by a few regents to scare candidate Carol Harter into opting out of the finalist interview process; second, to tell Jim Rogers what I thought of his efforts to disparage the board to position himself as the white knight coming to the rescue.

I called his office, scheduled a breakfast meeting for the following day, and booked my flight. Vice chair of the board at the time, I felt that my fears of his using the press to advance his personal agenda were confirmed and this was not a good start to a working partnership. I had been trained and served as a consultant for the Association of Governing Boards of Universities and Colleges (AGB) for several years and was clear about what constitutes a positive board-chancellor relationship. Trashing the board in the press is not a "best practice."

I found Rogers at his reserved table in his favorite breakfast hangout. I barely knew him, but I didn't care. Parking myself at his table, I leaned forward and said, "What the hell do you think you are doing?" (I used a stronger four-letter word than "hell," but at this late stage hate to tarnish my image as an advocate for decorum in public office).

He was taken aback as I continued to vent my anger at what I saw as his careless disregard for the reputation of Nevada's higher education system. We had a good group of regents at the time. Steve Sisolak, Mike Wixom, Stavros Anthony, Bret Whipple, Thalia Dondero, Dorothy Gallagher, James Dean Leavitt, Doug Hill, and Howard Rosenberg, among others, were all thoughtful, smart, conscientious elected officials who cared about Nevada's colleges and universities. We were all willing and ready to work with our new interim chancellor, but calling people names in the press was not constructive. I knew that bashing the board could have legislative and economic consequences—who would give us the funding we requested if they believed we were the incompetents he had made us out to be?

To my surprise, Rogers listened to everything I had to say. I don't know what I expected his reaction would be, and I didn't care, but receptive hadn't occurred to me. I cared about the board, which he had publicly attacked, and its reputation. In terms of tough talk, I was impressed that he could take it as well as dish it out. He seemed to admire me for having flown down from the north to give him hell. This odd exchange launched a positive relationship, one that Jim and I developed in the years that followed. We violently disagreed at times, and I held back nothing in speaking my mind in the kind of language that I learned made an impression on him. In the end, he at times wound up taking my advice.

Regarding his memo, I didn't disagree with some of the charges he made, and I looked tentatively forward to his new eyes on our functioning, and a constructive conversation. Reputation matters, however, and is an invaluable asset in any enterprise. The reputation of colleges and universities must be guarded as central to their well-being and not treated as expendable in the pursuit of someone's agenda. Whatever the board's shortcomings, and whatever public pushback resulted from controversial decisions, publicly berating the board was undeserved, mean-spirited, and counterproductive. During my entire three-term tenure on the board, a majority of regents served honorably and conscientiously. Enough of us with multiterm experience provided historical memory and context for difficult decisions, and enough respected thought leaders who were clear of personal agendas maintained decorum.

When I compare the board in those years with the 2021–22 Board of Regents, who are embroiled in a messy public dispute and a formal complaint by the chancellor against board leadership, our disagreements seem minor, civil, and tame. Higher education board dynamics can be contentious because big decisions are being made with many different stakeholders, most importantly the public, looking on. Board governance is not designed, nor well-served, if recommendations by administrators are rubber stamped and debate is suppressed. It is important to balance the need to vigorously debate policy matters with maintaining a sensitivity to public perceptions. Retaining public confidence and protecting the reputation of colleges and universities are part of the role of being a regent. Public airing of internal disputes, as is currently occurring in NSHE, brings only disrepute.

My biggest confrontation with Chancellor Rogers was when he singled out President Harter of UNLV for harassment and criticized her leadership and relationships with donors. I still have a file of the memoranda that flew between them, and in my view, he was brutal, always delivering censure in his preferred hyperbolic tone. It was clear to many that Harter's ten years of leadership had brought significant advancement to UNLV. Her accomplishments have been publicly noted and lauded. It occurred to me, as a burr under Jim's saddle, that he listened to a few critics, who usually referenced style not substance, drew a judgment, and rode with it. Having chaired the search committee that brought Harter to UNLV a decade before, I was not going to allow her to be driven out. The chancellor and I butted heads and had tough words. I have in the same file that contains some of their heated exchanges a handwritten note from Jim on lined paper that reads:

"Jill, As I have respectfully told you, I have not ever nor [do I] now have any intention of firing Carol Harter. You have my word that no such action will take place as long as I am Chancellor. James E. Rogers."

Harter resigned a year after that memo. One can draw one's own conclusions.

Chancellor Rogers was also not a fan of President John Lilley of UNR, who did not try to work well with President Harter when he came onboard in 2001, in contrast to what his long-serving and popular predecessor Joe Crowley had done. Crowley, with his convivial humor, smart politics, and good nature got along well with almost everyone and was admired throughout the system. Chancellor Rogers was also aware of the UNR female faculty's opposition to Lilley's presidency, which was brought out in his performance review, and he also saw shortcomings to his style of leadership. This may have figured into Lilley's resignation the year after Chancellor Rogers came onboard.

A major source of conflict between Chancellor Rogers and the board was his failure to recognize the limits of his delegated authority. He never reconciled himself to the fact of who works for whom, and that the regents are the final authority in NSHE, not the chancellor. The board, for its part, in the early days of Rogers's tenure, made the mistake of granting him the power to hire and fire presidents. Such high-impact decisions must be carefully considered in effective governance since leadership is so pivotal to the progress and well-being of colleges and universities, and since transitions are uncertain and disruptive. A thoughtful, consultive process of review is important in gauging the performance of sitting presidents. Consultation wasn't this chancellor's usual way of doing business though, and some of his more viscerally based decisions didn't turn out well. Rogers second-guessed his chosen replacement for Harter and later recommended that he be fired. His choice for the CSN president, Richard Carpenter, followed a similar trajectory.

After I stepped off the board in 2006, one kerfuffle involved Chancellor Rogers going a step too far in stretching his bounds of authority. It was hardly a first occurrence, but one in which the regents drew a line in the sand. Rogers threatened to resign if Regent James Dean Leavitt, elected to the board in 2004, was put forward for board chair or vice chair. Leavitt's sin was disagreeing publicly with the chancellor. This time, Rogers's encroachment on regents' authority was unacceptable. A chancellor dictating which regents the board selects as their leaders is outside his administrative lane of authority. The board is the final authority, not the chancellor, who is an employee, and who serves at the pleasure of the board.

Board chair Bret Whipple did the right thing by not caving into Chancellor Rogers's demand, resulting in a two-word letter from Rogers to Whipple, "I resign." Three days later, he changed his mind and withdrew his resignation. Leavitt did go on to serve commendably in board leadership.

Jim Rogers had strong likes and dislikes and did not suffer fools lightly. He could be mercurial and sharp-tongued, but beyond the bluster was a good and decent human being with good intentions. Whatever else might be said of his management style, he was endlessly generous, had a big heart, and gave a lot of his wealth to advance education, which he cared about deeply. Beyond his large gift to the University of Arizona College of Law, subsequently named after him, he gave large gifts to Nevada's institutions as well.

His largesse was especially appreciated by a few dozen higher education and policy leaders from around the country who had come into his orbit. For several years during his tenure as Nevada's chancellor, he organized and fully paid for a gathering of these leaders and friends at the Sonora Resort, a luxury property on the eastern coast of Vancouver Island, Canada. Seaplanes flew us out from Seattle, Washington, for this rich, rewarding three-day experience. Salmon fishing in the morning was followed by policy discussions in the afternoon and the free-flowing exchange of ideas over supper. I'm not sure I was on the invitation list until after my tough Vegas breakfast encounter with Jim, which seemed to earn me his respect.

Jim stepped down in 2009 after five years as chancellor. Dan Klaich followed as the system's next chancellor. Klaich had a long history of connection to Nevada's higher education system and a good understanding of regent politics. He had served two terms as a northern Nevada regent from 1983 to 1997, returning seven years later, when Rogers appointed him general counsel for NSHE. He then was promoted to executive vice chancellor under Rogers until Rogers's resignation.

Klaich's seven-year tenure as chancellor was longer than the three chancellors he succeeded—Jarvis, Nichols, and Rogers. His competence, sociability, and knowledge of system history served the regents well. The years of his leadership were marked by growth of the institutions and relative calm on the governance front. The regents accepted his resignation reluctantly in 2016 after a brouhaha with legislative leaders, who felt they had been misled. The years since his departure have seen more controversy and efforts by legislative leaders to move to an appointed, rather than elected, board of regents.

Klaich was a mentor to me when I first was elected to the board in 1988 and when I felt flummoxed by the existing alliances and undercurrents of undisclosed agendas. Also, I learned later, not every board member wanted to see me elected—particularly one. Coming onto an established body of sitting officials takes some sorting out: you have to find your footing to navigate the political currents of personal agendas and preferences. Regents are expected to govern with equal care for all institutions in the system, but favorites and biases are inevitable given individual histories and Nevada's dispersed geography. The distance between Las Vegas and Elko covers hundreds of miles of desert, and culturally speaking they are as different as Earth and Mercury. It was obvious to me that Klaich was knowledgeable about the ways of the board and could be a trusted advisor. His good counsel was invaluable as I learned how to navigate a political office and policy role that was completely foreign territory to me. By my second and third terms as regent, I, like Klaich, was mentoring those who followed.

It is ironic to fast-forward two decades and encounter one of the most recent and stunning examples of a chancellor/board rupture that NSHE has encountered. In an unprecedented move in fall 2021, the sitting chancellor, Melody Rose, issued a twenty-one-page complaint against two members of the Board of Regents, the chair and vice chair, claiming they had created a hostile workplace for her. It read, in part:

> Through this memorandum I am providing evidence of a hostile work environment on the basis of my sex: persistent hostility, abuse of power, consistent undermining, and multiple violations of Board of Regents (BOR) Handbook and policy, as well as my own contract. Combined, these abuses interfere with my obligation to discharge my responsibilities as articulated in the Bylaws, policies, and my contract. I respectfully request immediate relief from these violations and will cooperate fully with any investigation into these allegations you deem appropriate.

The complaint was directed to the NSHE's general counsel's office but was subsequently leaked to the press. It became a highly charged issue that attracted national press attention and played out in the Nevada press over the following weeks and months.

Again, tension between board members and the system or institution head are not unprecedented, neither in Nevada nor the rest of the country, but aspects of this 2021 development were highly unusual.

In twenty years of doing consulting work on university governance around the country, I have never encountered a system head issuing a formal complaint through legal channels against the leaders of the board, who are essentially her bosses. Given that institution and system heads serve at the pleasure of the boards they represent, expectations of the chain of authority weigh against it. The Nevada case may well set a precedent about whether an institutional leader making such charges against a board or board members can persist in that position. As is often the case in these instances of board-chancellor (or board-president) divisions, the size of the faction of board members who become disenchanted is often a deciding factor. During my tenure, it wasn't necessarily a majority of regents that set in motion a resignation, but rather a significant group of influential regents who signaled their loss of confidence in the individual. Often chancellors or presidents who discern the lack of support with an influential faction of a board begin making transition plans themselves.

The most striking aspect of this Nevada case was the agency Chancellor Rose felt to call out her bosses on charges of sexual discrimination. The long overdue #MeToo movement has finally tilted the playing field to allow women to be heard and taken seriously when making such charges. What a difference three decades makes! As a new regent in the early nineties, I had initiated and led NSHE's first effort to assess gender discrimination against women in our colleges and universities. The sexual harassment women faculty and students faced was a major finding of the surveys we conducted—and one of the targets of our recommendations for remediation.

Thirty years ago, women had no agency to either complain of mistreatment or expect any consequence of their action, other than likely retaliation against them. Chancellor Rose's complaint has invited much support from women around the state, including a gathering in her honor hosted by the former mayor of Las Vegas, Jan Jones Blackhurst. It was also probably instrumental in creating the space for Truckee Meadows Community College's president, Karin Hilgersom, in a follow-up action, to issue a similar complaint against several regents. What a leap forward in women's rights these actions represent.

Another unusual aspect of this standoff between Chancellor Rose and board leaders was that it played out in the public. The complaint was clearly a personnel matter. The twenty-one-page document issued by the chancellor was sent to the NSHE counsel's office, which followed up by hiring outside counsel to investigate the charges. In every other setting I have encountered in higher education governance, these matters are handled and settled internally. Personnel matters are one of a few areas of public university deliberations which can be, and almost always are, handled outside of the public view. That this matter was leaked and played out in the Nevada and national press was not only highly unusual but also damaging to the entire system of Nevada's colleges and universities. Colleges and universities depend existentially on drawing students to their campuses, and events that diminish their carefully managed brands hurt those efforts.

As Shakespeare said in *Othello* of the power of reputation: "Who steals my purse steals trash; 'tis something, nothing; 'twas mine, 'tis his, and has been slave to thousands; but he that filches from me my good name robs me of that which not enriches him and makes me poor indeed."

In fall 2021, an outside investigation was launched into the charges Chancellor Rose leveled against board leadership. While the resulting report did point to "uncivil behavior" on the part of some board members and an "inappropriate professional environment," it did not substantiate the charges of sex-based discrimination and a hostile workplace. Chancellor Rose's resignation followed.

One of the differences I have noted between the regents with whom I served and more recent electees is that they haven't had the time to learn the challenge of balancing regents' authority with that of the chancellor and presidents, whom they appoint. Boards do best when they delegate authority to manage institutions to chancellors and presidents and monitor their performance in systematic ways but get into trouble when they step outside their governance lane and micromanage, second-guessing the leaders they have appointed.

The training and education of new board members is critical in helping them to understand that as citizen trustees of colleges and universities their job is not to run institutions, but as fiduciaries, to support, oversee, and advance their well-being. The devil is in the details of understanding the distinction between governance and management, which is not always clear-cut to newcomers. Learning how to navigate those parallel lanes of authority takes guidance and time.

One of the "best practices" of those of us who consult with boards to enhance their performance is having regular training and continuous education sessions, wherein boards have opportunities to evaluate their own performance. Another best practice is the importance of open communication lines between boards and their appointed leaders. Good communication engenders trust, a vital component in an effective board-chancellor relationship. When communication falls short, the opportunity for disharmony can follow. This principle seems to have played a role in the widely publicized board-chancellor dispute that rocked NSHE in 2021.

The history of Nevada's higher education system is full of triumphs, challenges, and struggles, particularly at the leadership level. Over the past decades, Nevada colleges and universities have grown and thrived in ways not seen in other states. Many outstanding presidents of our institutions deserve kudos. The Board of Regents, despite its tempestuous reputation, rightfully gets credit for system successes as well. In fairness, the board tends to receive more public notice when things go wrong than when things go right. Negative stories create newsworthy press, but rarely do we hear about the hundreds of hours regents spend in meetings listening to reports and proposals, and attending numerous events, all to do what is right for the Nevada's colleges and universities. Unlike legislators and other constitutional officers in the state, regents are not paid for their service. Their time and effort are compensated only by a sense of making a difference for the students of Nevada and for the many ways NSHE institutions advance the status and opportunities of its citizens.

It is not easy to sum up such a long involvement in office as a Nevada regent, and one in which I was such a novice at the start. I experienced highs and lows, stresses and triumphs, knowing that the actions and policies I debated had huge impacts on colleges and universities, their faculty, and students. During my tenure, I served with many thoughtful and committed colleagues whom I liked, admired, and respected for their dedication to the worthy enterprise they served. The work ethic that bound us was one of unpaid service to the high calling of education—a calling that rises above all others in its ability to make the biggest difference in the lives of individuals, communities, and our nation.

I served during a time when legislative funding for the system was less and less secure—but when all Nevada's higher education institutions were growing. Our state has long had a low college-going rate and a low graduation rate compared with states that have better fiscal support, and I loved being part of the policy team determined to change those statistics. Running and winning in that first election to the Board of Regents in 1988, I didn't know that being in "the room where it happens" would prove so deeply satisfying, challenging, and rewarding. I did not envision that two decades as a regent would lead to so many other opportunities to make a difference in the higher education landscape of the United States and beyond.

I'm aware of the time and commitment I brought to my job as regent, and of the many tough votes I cast. I'm proud to say I never missed a board meeting, regardless of other demands and the time away from my family it entailed. My family and I did enjoy some perks: We liked being in the President's Box at UNR and UNLV football games. President Harter shared her tickets to the National Finals Rodeo in Las Vegas with us every year, which Steve, being from a ranching family, especially enjoyed. An unparalleled memory was our overnight stay in Regent Lonnie Hammargren's amazing and semi-bizarre museum home in Las Vegas. I'm not sure what surprised us most—his planetarium, his life-sized dinosaur skeleton, or the fact that he appeared early the first morning of our stay awakening us by our bed with a tray of coffee and treats. What a host and colleague!

Many of us forged friendships and socialized together while serving during those more collegial years on the Board of Regents. Shelley Berkley and I formed a lifelong friendship, and I have often been a guest at her Las Vegas home. Carolyn Sparks and Thalia Dondero were also good friends. I formed a special bond with Doug Seastrand's delightful and talented family. They stayed over with us at our Tahoe home one summer and welcomed our son, Ryan, into their home on his drives to Austin, Texas, where he pursued his PhD in math. The Seastrands, a talented musical family, and I joined in their songfests around a piano. My friendship with Howard Rosenberg continues to this day. I have a favorite picture of the regents' meeting at the UNR campus where he ferried President Harter and me on his motor scooter in a hair-raising ride across campus to an event.

For many years, I hosted a dinner for all the regents, presidents, and senior staff on the deck of our Lake Tahoe home. It was a welcome break and opportunity to relate socially as *people* instead of as titles at our board meetings. Chatting beneath the pines and sharing a bottle of wine as the waves lapped and hues shifted in the setting sun was a tonic from tense discussion and close votes. We may never see the good old days of getting to know each other outside of the board room again, as the tone of discourse in all elective settings has grown so rancorous and unfriendly. Sometimes when I walk the shore at Tahoe now, I sense something invaluable has been lost.

CHAPTER 6

Back on the Trail Again

In 2005, as my third term as regent wound down and the turbulent years of Jim Rogers's tenure as chancellor rolled on, I had no specific plans. The option of running for a fourth term existed, but I wondered if I had settled too comfortably into a passive role. As the longest-serving regent at that time, I worried that I had come to rely on acting from my eighteen years of experience in familiar territory rather than pursuing new routes that would align with my passion for innovative improvement.

While in this undecided state, I began getting calls from the head of the Democratic Congressional Campaign Committee (DCCC), Representative Rahm Emanuel of Illinois. He was suggesting that I run for Congress in Nevada's open Second Congressional District, being vacated by Jim Gibbons as he set off to run for governor.

"Who, me?" was my startled, genuine response.

District 2 at that time included most of Nevada, except primarily Democratic Clark County. Emanuel, as the DCCC's head, was responsible for recruiting and supporting Democratic candidates in the 2006 election cycle, and he was not one to take "no" for an answer.

I wasn't sure then how my name had been put forward to the DCCC. I learned later that because I had won three competitive regent races in Nevada's conservative Republican north, people saw me as someone with campaign experience, name recognition, and a record of electoral success. All true, but in my calculation, Emanuel knew that the fate of Democratic candidates in Nevada's Second Congressional District seemed sealed: none had ever won. History lined up against Democrats in that mostly rural two-thirds of the state. He kept calling though, weekly; and I kept resisting, explaining how the partisan odds would be impossible to overcome. Winning an election, I had learned, is much more satisfying than losing one.

If I began to waver in my resistance to Emanuel's persuasion, it was in remembering similar claims I'd made decades earlier about my chances of winning a Douglas County legislative race: "Who, me? No way—the odds are stacked in favor of Republicans."

I then went on to almost win that race.

Another reason I always picked up the phone when I saw Emanuel's "202" Washington, DC, prefix flashing was that I felt strongly about our disastrous American foreign policy in the Middle East. Two years earlier, the US had invaded Iraq on false intelligence, which left me outraged. I had lived, worked, and traveled in the Middle East, and I knew and liked the region immensely. War becomes personal when you know people residing in countries being torn apart as weapons of war are unleashed. I was disturbed that so few in leadership positions in the United States recognized the false justifications offered for attacking Iraq. Too few had the courage to speak up in opposition to the political groundswell fueled by unfounded reports of weapons of mass destruction. Iraq looked like another falsely grounded US war target that I had protested in the early seventies—Vietnam.

After living abroad in my late twenties and traveling widely ever since, I've closely followed and frequently discussed US foreign policy. For years, I could not find many others in my Nevada orbit who shared my interest and concern for the rest of the world. I was often frustrated by the recognition that America's geographical isolation, bordered by two large oceans, limited our citizens' opportunities to meet, interact with, and come to know people from other countries and cultures. This geography, along with our nation's unique history, has bred an insularity and apathy about what happens beyond our shores. To counteract this disconnect, I have given hundreds of cross-cultural and world-events talks. Building international insight and cross-cultural understanding has been a major commitment of mine for decades. Having an anthropologist worldview made helping fellow Nevadans see the common humanity that binds people across national boundaries as key to building a world that works for everyone.

In pondering Emanuel's appeal to run for the Nevada's open congressional seat, I knew I could offer a much-needed perspective to foreign policy deliberations, particularly about the Middle East, whose language I knew and whose culture I understood. This was the sort of useful contribution I was seeking to make, one that in retrospect I could see I had been working toward for many years. The daunting realities of such a political race, however, kept me firmly on the sidelines.

"It isn't winnable," I told Emanuel as his calls persisted through the spring of 2005.

He was clever: he had others call me as well—names I knew. Once, returning from a trip to Vegas, I checked my phone messages: "Hi, Jill. This is John Kerry. I'd like to talk to you about serving our country at a time it needs you. Call me back, and we can talk." Halfway through listening to the message, I stopped in my tracks. "Holy cow, Senator John Kerry is calling me!"

Emanuel was intent on persuading me to get in the race, but I continued to believe it was not winnable.

So it went, through the spring, and when summer arrived, he made a request I found hard to turn down. He asked that I come to Washington, DC, to simply meet with other members of Congress, particularly women, who had won in Republican districts.

"No commitment, just come, meet, and listen," he assured me.

Unable to find grounds to refuse and inspired by the idea of meeting with members of Congress, I booked my ticket. My dear friend Representative Shelley Berkley, with whom I served on the Nevada Board of Regents, offered a bedroom in her DC home.

Visiting Washington, DC, and Capitol Hill inspires a certain reverence. The marble statues and monuments seen everywhere reflect the symbolic meaning the city holds for all US citizens and remind visitors that they are on sacred ground. Approaching the congressional offices that Emanuel had scheduled me to visit, I felt a tinge of awe. My first meeting was in the impressive and expansive office of Nancy Pelosi, the California representative who was the minority leader at the time (she would become Speaker of the House in 2006). She was encouraging, warm, and resolute about retaking the House of Representatives in 2006. I had other meetings with congresswomen from Republican districts and then lunch with Democratic luminaries James Carville and Paul Begala. It was a heady schedule of meetings with political notables who had been prompted to encourage me to run for the Nevada seat. As much as I enjoyed the opportunity and rush of attention, I felt uneasy because I still was not in a very persuadable frame of mind.

"How did it go?" Steve asked when I returned. "Is the arm-twisting getting stronger?"

"It was exciting and flattering to be so sought after," I replied. "I would love to be there, love to run, if I could see a way to overcome the political odds, but I can't see it. If we lived in Las Vegas with its Democratic majority, I'd launch today, feeling certain I could add a needed voice to the political conversation in Washington. But solidly Republican rural Nevada electing a Democratic woman is hard to fathom."

That July, Steve and I took our twentysomething-year-old kids, Ryan and Tobyn, on a trip to Greece and Italy. We took a cruise around the Greek islands and on those blue waters, catching sunsets and sunrises, nobody could reach me. My joy in traveling was rekindled. Returning to the Mediterranean with my family, where I had spent time years before, made it all the more special. One of the side trips we took on the Greek mainland was to the ancient site of Delphi, which reached its peak of political influence in the fourth and fifth centuries BC. Many seeking prophetic guidance visited the Oracle of Apollo at Delphi to seek political advice. Standing at that mountainous site of ancient prophesy, I wished there were still an oracle there to whisper in my ear.

Visiting Greece was one of many foreign adventures Steve and I enjoyed over the years with our kids. Raising them in a parochial, rural environment, albeit a beautiful one, I was determined that they experience the wider world and feel comfortable in it. Thus, our days of family travel abroad began early in their lives. Whatever else filled the calendar, I always made sure to prioritize our trips abroad.

I had barely unpacked when Emanuel called with a new proposal: Would I come to DC in later August for an Emily's List training for progressive women House and Senate candidates?

"I don't qualify under the 'candidate' label," I reminded him.

I hadn't made that decision, but he urged me nonetheless to accept the invitation and join the company of other women who had taken the leap.

"You'll get a sense of what's required to be a successful candidate," he said.

Again, it was a hard invitation to turn down. I love being around women who choose to play big and knew I would enjoy spending three days with them in a program designed by Emily's List, one of the most renown and respected national organizations for supporting promising women candidates. I knew Emanuel had arranged the invitation hoping to nudge my "undecided" status into the "decided" category.

At yet another exhilarating DC experience, I attended session after session with a group of accomplished women, women who had already committed to running for the US Senate or House. Front and center when it came to media coaching and fundraising training, they welcomed rigorous public speaking practice and feedback. No one blinked an eye at critique, and no one took things personally—you learn not to, when so much is at stake. These women were all up to something larger than themselves and were eager to acquire the skills necessary to be successful candidates.

An easy sense of camaraderie bonded us. Whatever political backgrounds we came from, the heady sense of stepping into a bigger game infused our spirits with energy, collegiality, and enthusiasm. Even though I was the lone undecided participant in the exercises, I was all-in and played full-out to learn everything I could about becoming an effective candidate on the national stage—just in case. Although I had media experience already, the one-on-one mock interview sessions in DC taught me how to react quickly and pivot the discussion if asked questions I felt unprepared to answer.

Despite the incredible enthusiasm and support I felt among the women at the Emily's List DC event, I continued to feel that the odds in my potential race were more daunting than they were for others. I wished the deck were stacked differently, and I kept pushing off making the commitment to run. My fellow participants that weekend understood my hesitation, given the lopsided partisan registration of my district and the obstacles I would face if I chose to go for it. I'm sure it made several of them feel more positive about their own races, races with more advantageous political demographics. Still, many said I would make a great candidate and encouraged me to stay open to changing my mind. I felt sad as the training came to an end and glum over the wedge I felt in being the lone holdout of the team Emily's List had pulled together.

At the final send-off celebratory dinner, a well-known keynote speaker with political credentials sought to build on the energy in the room and cheer us on.

I don't remember her name, but she referenced President Kennedy's famous line, "Ask not what your country can do for you—ask what you can do for your country." She spoke about how the peril and challenge of the times call forth the leaders the nation needs, and how the times we are living through speak directly to those in the room who have answered the call. In closing, she referenced a 2004 commencement speech given by Ted Sorensen, the former speech writer for President Kennedy: "Future historians studying the decline and fall of America will mark this as the time the tide began to turn—toward a mean-spirited mediocrity in place of a noble beacon."

Something about the tide turning flashed a clear visual image and struck a deep chord in me. Decline—not on my watch. I jumped up and announced to the room, "Okay, everyone, I'm in!"

The group cheered and rushed over to congratulate me.

As farewells were being exchanged, I thought, "What have I just done? Should I pull back this pledge?" And then, my phone rang. Emanuel was on the other end.

"Congratulations, Jill, we've got the press release out and are delighted you made the right choice."

Press release? I was stunned. My think-it-through window vanished. Somewhat dazed, I could manage only to say, "I think I better call my husband."

Walking back to my hotel room, I ruminated, "What have I done?"

Too late: nothing to do now but figure out how to chart a course ahead. Just as I had fallen backward into a Nevada legislative race three decades earlier, I had leapt toward the new and unknown.

Emanuel suggested I stay in DC an extra day to meet with the DCCC team, which helps candidates identify a campaign manager and begin the nuts and bolts of building a campaign team. He introduced me to David Hamrick, who headed the 2005 DCCC team supporting candidates, and his help was very supportive and reassuring to me. We spent time together at his office and he laid out the next steps, making it sound all doable and assuring me of the DCCC's help and support.

The first order of business would be hiring a campaign manager. Hamrick introduced me to a couple of potentials, but the chemistry didn't feel right. A few other meetings left me with the realization that I had entered a whole new world of national campaign politics, about which I knew next to nothing. My feelings replicated those of my ERA days in Nevada when I said, "Okay, I'll run," also facing the prospect of knowing zilch about what I had stepped into. To be honest, I have often liked the excitement of the unknown, but running for Congress felt like the highest stakes "unknown" I had faced yet.

I returned to Nevada to convince my family that my new adventure would be one we would share—and to figure out how to rearrange my life to make it all work. Hamrick sent me the CV of a third campaign manager prospect, and after a promising conversation on the phone, he and I agreed to an in-person interview. David Cohen was a twentysomething Brown University graduate from Massachusetts who had worked in several campaigns on the East Coast but never as a campaign manager. We decided that he should fly out to Nevada so we could try each other out.

Our first encounter leaving the Reno airport sealed the deal. I had the latest Harry Potter book on cassette tape sitting on the passenger seat. I was a devoted Harry Potter fan and loved to listen to the books on tape when I drove. It turned out David was an equally devoted fan, and our first twenty minutes of conversation was all Hogwarts. There is a special chemistry that arises between readers who share the love of books and the stories that most engage them. The Harry Potter series brought that sense of connection and camaraderie out between readers in spades. David related to Harry, whom I thought he looked like; and I related to Hermione, who was a Muggle like me and best at mastering magic. By the time David and I were back at the Gardnerville house, we were feeling encouraged that he and I could partner on this campaign and navigate its challenges together.

David was supposed to bunk in our separate studio apartment just for the weekend interview, but he stayed for the next several months. Our home is in the Carson Valley, on the side of the mountain that climbs west up to the Lake Tahoe Heavenly Valley ski resort. On the east side of our house and the studio apartment is a view across the verdant grazing fields of the valley. On the west side are numerous hillside trails that smell of sage and pine. David and I took many an afternoon hike to plot strategy. I cooked us grilled cheese sandwiches for lunch everyday so we could remain focused in-place on the outlines of the campaign ahead.

Our chemistry held and grew into friendship over the course of the fourteen-month campaign, as we often spent ten to twelve hours together every day. Joined at the hip in common cause, we became close. Being a campaign manager was new territory for David, as was the candidate role for me, and we developed an easy rapport in working together. He had a good network of colleagues from his previous campaign experience and began the process of planning, hiring, and putting together the blueprint that a congressional campaign demanded. In all those intense, focused, and often stressful months, we found time to joke, laugh, and have fun together.

We formally issued a press release announcing the campaign in mid-September. David made two terrific hires in Chelsea Peterson for data analysis, scheduling, and everything else, and Ellie Highstreet for communication. Both women were from South Dakota. My job was to start raising the thousands of dollars we would need to fund campaign over the months ahead. We converted the studio apartment David had occupied into campaign headquarters while he, Chelsea, and Ellie moved to a nearby rental.

Fundraising, the key to a large-scale political campaign, is the primary responsibility of the candidate. Learning of the sums that it would take to play to win, I wasn't sure I had the chops. My regent races in Washoe, Carson, Douglas, Storey, and Lyon (my district) allowed a budget in the low five figures. The million to a million-and-a-half goal put before me seemed beyond attainable. The Emily's List training had focused on fundraising skills, so I knew the fundamentals: when asking people for campaign contributions, ask for specific amounts above what you think they might be able to contribute, knowing you can always negotiate down. A stumbling block for me was my upbringing—as a child, I had learned that asking for money was beyond the pale. Not in the habit of asking others for much, let alone money, I had a store of personal resistance to get over in short order.

Any serious candidate will tell you that fundraising is not the most fun element of running a campaign, but it is the most critical. With Toni Kendall, an executive coach I knew who came on board to help with fundraising, I learned to shift my mental context from one of asking for money to one of asking for support in the goal of electing a Democrat in Nevada's Second Congressional District for the first time. Opening a call with such an impressive—if not lofty sounding—dream, made calls easier for me. I also enjoyed talking politics and getting the perspective of others, over the phone and in person. Seeing the monetary sums adding up as the various reporting deadlines rolled in gave me a rush of pride. The DCCC took notice when in the first weeks of my candidacy I raised more than $200,000 and later down the track, when the press reported I was outraising my opponents on the Republican side of the race by a considerable margin.

David networked to identify a couple of talented national campaign professionals in media and campaign materials who flew out for a weekend huddle to plot campaign messaging and strategy. We met at our family's Tahoe house for a couple of days as I laid out my life history and they listened to identify the narrative themes they felt would resonate in Nevada. Our home in Glenbrook sits close to the lake and lies on several acres my grandparents, Charles and Mary Derby, purchased in 1937. We have kept the house much as they built it, with needed renovations. The library my grandparents assembled, of late-nineteenth and early-twentieth-century books, greets every visitor. The granite fireplace has seen almost a century of family gatherings. This cherished home made a great setting for plotting a Nevada congressional campaign.

Our campaign advisors kept circling back to the fact that I was born on the Flying Flapjack Ranch in Lovelock, a fact that would work as a grounding connection to my ranching roots in a district that was predominately rural. That I was young when we left the ranch for my father's wartime flying service was not an obstacle to the construction of the brand. (I had a hard time getting my head around that I was a brand!) I had only thought of branding in terms

of cattle and quickly saw that I was out of my wheelhouse of competence, much as I had been the first time I dove into political waters.
Once again, I was playing over my head and grateful for the advice
of my young and professional team.

"Start with the passion and figure out the details later" seemed
to be my modus vivendi.

The logistics of my campaign were formidable. In that first decade
of the twenty-first century, Nevada's Second Congressional District
encompassed a territory of more than one hundred thousand miles,
including almost all of Nevada except for Las Vegas. When I mentioned those numbers to fellow candidates running in dense congressional districts in the East, their eyes rolled in disbelief. Clark County,
with Las Vegas, accounts for almost three-fourths of the state's population with the remaining one-fourth dispersed in small towns over a
broad expanse of desert. Nevada is known as the "Sagebrush State"
for good reason. Walking the district and knocking on doors were
not going to be in the script; even thinking of driving around gave
me palpitations. Detailing how to efficiently align my schedule with
these desert distances was in the hands of my campaign team. In an
uncomfortable release of control over the timing of my own life, I
turned my calendar over to David. Reno, with its several hundred
thousand residents, was central to our strategy, particularly given
the presence of the University of Nevada, Reno, where my multiyear
tenure on the Board of Regents was best known.

Political wisdom dictated that the rural countries could not be
ignored in a race encompassing fifteen of the state's seventeen counties, but the ratio of overwhelming Republican voter registration in
those fifteen rural counties had to be factored in. Midway through
our campaign, two seasoned pilots with small airplanes, Peter Neu-
mann and Robert Chester, offered their services, which turned out
to be not only time-saving but fun.

I had seen Nevada from the air years before, when shortly after
marrying Steve and moving to Gardnerville I took flying lessons at
Minden Airport. My first solo flight was to Derby Field in Lovelock,
on land that had belonged to my great grandfather. On that flight, I
landed, told the airport staff of my relationship to the "Derby" name,
and flew onto Elko. My return flight went awry. I lost my sense of
direction and navigation over the seemingly endless desert with no

clear markings. Feeling alarmed, I climbed higher to call in to the Reno control tower to get my bearings. The experience was totally humiliating, but it gave me a glimpse of the great Nevada desert from several thousand feet up and I learned an important lesson. As a follow-up, my flight instructor chastised me for my screwup, letting me know that male pilots are more likely to make navigational errors that lead to serious outcomes than women because men are more reluctant than women to admit they are lost.

It could have been an even more embarrassing experience if I had set down, as the Reno tower suggested, in Lovelock. The day was hot, the air bumpy, and my mouth dry from my alarm of not knowing if I was on course. Thirsty and nervous, I took a gulp of water from my thermos, which missed my mouth with an air bounce and landed on my lap. Following the advice of the Reno tower, I prepared to land at Lovelock and called in my plane ID number on my approach. As I descended to one hundred feet, I glanced at my wet lap and horrified by what people would think, frantically yanked the plane nose up and headed back to Minden.

I was happy to be back in a small plane with someone else in the cockpit. Some of the far-flung excursions my campaign team and I took to distant rural corners of the state for annual parades and festivities are among my fondest memories. The best way to connect with a town of populations in the hundreds is when they all gather on Main Street for a special occasion. We laid out a year's calendar around these events particularly over the summer and fall of 2006, when so many were traditionally held. Much of rural Nevada is too cold in the winter for outside gatherings.

Out of our many flying visits to distant small towns such as Elko, Ely, and Battle Mountain, the one to Wells was particularly memorable. Wells, near the northern Nevada-Utah border, is home to about one thousand residents. A small group of supporters had scheduled an event there, but at the last minute, the date had been changed and we hadn't gotten the memo. I was with my trusty, upbeat campaign sidekick, Cindy Trigg.

As a candidate, I was never scheduled to go anywhere alone. Cindy, in her first political campaign, was my "body person," as campaign terminology defined the role. She was always by my side, carrying my purse and campaign materials, taking notes, writing down names for follow-up, and generally taking care of my needs, including providing food and being a sounding board when needed. Cindy was terrific in her role. Once in Wells, after discovering the scheduling error, we resolved to make the best use of our allotted time by walking the main streets—there were only a couple. Because I enjoyed the "introducing myself" element of campaigning, Cindy and I figured dropping in on stores and businesses might be a win-win adventure. I had seen how a stranger—a woman—or two, seemed to offer something different, something to interrupt the daily routine.

After an hour of meeting and greeting, Cindy and I noticed a restaurant near Highway 80 with a bright neon sign that read, "Bella's Café." It was a small place, but it seemed to be hopping with customers. Hoping they were locals who could vote, we went in and ordered two Diet Cokes. Scoping the place, I noticed that the six or seven tables were all occupied by single men, some with their sunglasses on, which seemed odd to me in the dim light of the café. Undeterred, I went to every table and introduced myself, reciting my usual spiel of running for Congress and asking if they were locals. I didn't get much of a response and found out that they were all from outside the area. They didn't seem to welcome my friendly approach, which was not the response I usually got. Cindy and I finished our drinks and left.

In the parking lot, we encountered a brightly dressed, well made-up, middle-aged woman who I thought might be the owner of the café, and thus a local voter. I stopped and asked, "Hi, are you Bella, by any chance?"

"Yes," she replied with a friendly smile.

Choosing to make the most of the occasion, I introduced myself, told her of my campaign, and asked her as I often did if there were particular issues that concerned her as a citizen of Nevada. She expounded on the need for better health care, particularly for rural women. I acknowledged her concern, offered my support and ideas for it, and continued in a discussion with her for several minutes more. As Cindy and I prepared to leave, I was delighted when Bella spoke up and offered to put one of my campaign signs in the café window. Feeling I had scored big time in my impulse to greet her outside the café, I told her we had a sign in the car and would bring it over. "Before you go," she said, "would you like a tour of the bordello?"

What?

Prostitution is legal in many rural counties in Nevada, and I had certainly seen red-light districts on several of my campaign swings. But none of the counties I spent time in—Douglas, Carson, Clark, and Washoe—had these establishments, so I was not used to seeing them. I struggled to keep my face from registering the shock of Bella's revelation. I managed a polite refusal of her tour offer, explaining we had to hurry along to stay on schedule. Cindy, quickly sizing up the potential political liability of a *"Derby for Congress"* sign in a bordello window—and possibly in my opponent's campaign ad—reminded me that we were "out of campaign signs" and suggested we have one delivered later.

We bid Bella adieu, keeping our composure until we could finally collapse in laughter at our ridiculous naivete at not being suspicious of an Elko County interstate café full of out-of-town men in dark glasses who did not warm to my approach to their tables. Cindy and I laughed all the way back to the plane, and our "near-scandal" became a source of great hilarity to our campaign team when we shared the news.

Parades were never my favorite events, but in rural Nevada they were a must-show. One thing that made them work well for me was that Chancellor Jim Rogers, who had become a good friend and was a strong supporter in my race, offered me cars out of his rare vintage car collection. He generously had them delivered to whatever location I planned to participate in a parade, from Pahrump, Mesquite, and Caliente in the south to Dayton, Fallon, and Winnemucca in the north. My favorite parade car he loaned us was a beautifully restored 1956 Chevrolet convertible with all the extra trimmings (worth about $125,000, we learned). It reminded me of a car that I loved to drive that I inherited from my aunt right out of college. He had it delivered to our house in Gardnerville for a clutch of close-by parades, and Steve was a nervous wreck that a pine cone might fall on it.

We had some memorable adventures getting to and from several remote parade locations along Nevada's eastern border: Alamo, Caliente, and Pioche all come to mind. At an annual barbecue near Alamo that my colleague Regent Bret Whipple's family hosted, I was invited to attend a football game later that evening, to the north, in Penaca.

David was with me on this excursion, and he and I decided to leave the game at halftime, after meeting and greeting parents of players and fans of both teams. As was typical, we got into an animated conversation before we had even turned onto the access road. It was our habit to recap the day's events and think ahead to what was next. We had a long late-night drive ahead of us, roughly seven hours back to Gardnerville, on the Nevada-California border. It was dark as we left Penaca, and because there are long distances between communities on Nevada's eastern edge, we drove along without roadside distraction, deep in campaign conversation.

I didn't notice any familiar landmarks, which by habit I began looking for after half an hour, but then I remembered that eastern Nevada was new territory to me. David checked the gas tank reading and suggested we stop for gas at the next opportunity. Stations can be few and far between in these desert expanses, and failing to pay attention can lead to breath-holding stretches of scouting for a gas pump. We passed a few scattered dark buildings, but no lights or signs suggested we were close to civilization.

Finally, we saw some lights and pulled into what turned out to be a shuttered gas station. As we swung back out to the road, I saw a sign just ahead, reading, "Welcome to Iron County." What! Oh, no. I groaned in disbelief.

"David, we're in the wrong state. There is no Iron County in Nevada!"

What a shock to discover that on our long journey back across Nevada to Gardnerville we had taken an hour's detour into Utah. For those who don't know the isolation of the western deserts and the far-between communities connected by simple two-lane roads, it might be hard to fathom how we could have driven the wrong way for so long into a neighboring state. We had taken a wrong turn when we first exited the football stadium, and since nothing had been familiar on the drive in, nothing contradicted it in the dark, on the way back out. We turned around in dismay at our strategic error and noticed the "Welcome to Utah" sign in the rearview mirror after retracing the thirty miles back to the Nevada border. We made it to Gardnerville at about three in the morning. I would like to say that keeping such hours was rare—it wasn't. Trying to cover one hundred thousand square miles of campaign territory in the time frame that back-to-back events could dictate required stretching stamina to it limits. Campaigning is a marathon, not a sprint.

Another memorable road trip adventure occurred one moon-less night across a broad reach of desert. We were traveling from a Fallon campaign rally to a next-day parade in Alamo, along a stretch of Nevada's famous Area 51 of flying saucer fame. A handful of the young, professional full-time staff on the campaign team were from the Midwest and East Coast. They had heard of this mysteri-ous extraterrestrial highway and knew of its flying saucer renown. Seven of us were traveling in two cars tandem. We took Highway 6 out of Tonopah and sometime past midnight came to the turnoff to Highway 375. A sign at this junction announces the beginning of extraterrestrial country where things might get strange.

We stopped the cars so that everyone could take pictures beside the sign. It was pitch-black as only Nevada desert nights can be, and in the spirit of fun I warned everyone to stick together, given the mys-terious unknowns attached to the area and the reputation of flying saucers abducting people. With the cars turned off, in the middle of nowhere, it was silent. The blackness was dramatic, unlike anything those coming from cities or even small towns had ever experienced. The stars stood out like sparkling diamonds over our heads. We had called a "time out" so that everyone could experience Nevada and its authentic desolation, and the night did not disappoint.

When someone suggested we all lie down in the middle of the darkened road to further admire and absorb the stars and the silence, our out-of-state contingent giggled. It seemed absurd, but there is no traffic on Nevada's deserted secondary roads at night and only the wandering desert cattle who cross these roads at their leisure pres-ent a hazard. We did it; we all lay down, and it was a magic moment in the otherwise rushed existence of a statewide political campaign.

The minutes ticked by. My son, Ryan, along to assist on this campaign swing, then whispered, "Mom, let's hide."

What fun! Three of us lying close by silently felt our way behind the front parked car and crouched in a ditch on the side of the road. Not long after, the rest of the group, who had been lying farther down the road near their car called out that they were ready to go. Silence.

"Hey, you guys, where are you?"

Silence. Whispered conversing. And then, "Come on, we know you're here. No one has been abducted. Ha ha ha."

They moved closer, but in the pitch-black we were well hidden. Lacking a flashlight, one of them suggested they light a match. Uh-oh: nervous they might set the sagebrush on fire, we gave ourselves up. Lighthearted interludes in what are often rushed, focused, and intense campaign trail efforts are as necessary as carrying drinking water in the desert.

For the next hour or so, Cindy drove our car white-knuckled across that unfenced federal range, dodging the desert cattle, to which frequent warning signs alert drivers. Twice, while I tried to grab a wink of sleep, we came over a rise or around a bend to a screeching halt, with a steer midroad lazily staring into our headlights. Our eastern colleagues noted these frightening near misses with disbelieving alarm.

It was gratifying how many people signed on as active supporters and came forward to help in various capacities. Some offered to host fundraising events in their homes, and many turned out to cheer us on at the many parades in which we participated. They showed up with cool water on hot summer parade days and offered to hand out fliers to distribute along the parade route. Local volunteers showed up in our campaign headquarters to prepare mailers with every shout-out. At times, more than twenty were in our campaign headquarters, addressing envelopes, licking, and stamping. Fellow Democrats and other supporters in towns all over Nevada offered their homes when we needed to stay over. Wherever and whatever the need, they continued to show up.

I was energized and inspired by all the people who care about elections and candidates and who participate wholeheartedly in choosing the government they want. Day after day, I witnessed democracy in action—the commitment of busy people finding time out in their lives to add their energy and talents to an election outcome. I was humbled as the candidate and even more committed to raising the funds to support the gallant efforts of so many people working to support our campaign and affect their federal government.

Being at the center of a group working in common cause with fervor and commitment is what makes the challenges surmountable

and worth it. The strong sense of bonding that occurs is more important than ever in our increasingly splintered and divided society.
My advice to all who want to experience giving part of themselves
over to a community for the greater good: if you don't want to run
yourself, sign up for the campaign of someone you believe in for an
important office, or sign on to a campaign for a cause that touches
your heart. The sense of synergy and esprit de corps that arises when
battling for a common goal is soul-stirring.

The confidence surrounding our campaign grew month after
month. One advantage we had was a lack of a serious primary. On
the Republican side, a primary pitted Nevada assemblywoman Shar-
ron Angle, Nevada secretary of state Dean Heller, former assemblywoman Dawn Gibbons, and others. David was quick to take
advantage of our ability to spend our money, introducing me to the
wider public and promoting my candidacy, while on the Republican
side they were spending theirs' attacking each other.

Our brilliant media advisor, Jason Ralston, saw that window
as an opportunity to "brand" me in the public mind—particularly
stressing my ranching roots and my early years on the Flying Flapjack Ranch in Lovelock. The TV ads Ralston wrote and directed
turned out to be wildly popular to a viewing public that was used
to attack ads featuring distorted faces of candidates in unflattering
poses. Our campaign took the high road instead, and one ad particularly resonated throughout the district and delighted television view-
ers who let us know. The ad showed Steve and me walking hand in
hand across a ranch corral. Steve pointed to a large cow pie in our
path and called out, "Watch your step!" to which I sidestepped and
replied, "Oh, there's a lot more of that in Washington!"

I loved adding that bit of humor to the branding message, and
people across the state played back that line to us for months to
come. Along parade routes, people would shout from the sidelines
while pointing to the road, "Watch your step!" We laughed. What
a concept, putting up an ad that made people smile and feel good
in an arena that usually has people diving for the remote and hitting the mute button.

The endorsement of Emily's List that summer brought in funds
from women around the country. It has always been a fact that it is
harder for women candidates to raise money for their campaigns,

so having this well-known and influential organization announce its support was a big boost. The DCCC, under Emanuel, had put our campaign on their Red to Blue list of promising races, which was another big boost that signaled not only its support but confidence that our race was playing strong against the odds in a challenging district. Funding from Emily's List and the DCCC helped bring in funds from other organizations as well. Our campaign especially prized these endorsements because our odds of winning were among the most daunting, and organizations target their endorsements according to odds of winning. We were being seen as a well-run race in a tough district with a good Democratic candidate. All this gave us more heart and determination to win.

David and I made the rounds of labor union headquarters in DC, meeting with their leaders in a request for funds. I had become a strong advocate for unions after watching the declining pay and benefits workers suffered in previous decades. I was all-in for the unions and the leveling effect they confer as corporations and owners have increased their leverage, wealth, and power.

Labor unions, however, were not familiar territory for me. No one in my family had belonged to a union, and I was way over my head in trying to grapple with the dizzying list of these organizations and their individual purpose and focus. The acronyms on the briefing papers David handed me left my head spinning: SEIU (Service Employees International Union), IBEW (International Brotherhood of Electrical Workers), UBC (United Brotherhood of Carpenters and Joiners of America), AFSCME (American Federation of State, County & Municipal Employees), and UFCWIU (United Food and Commercial Workers Union International). As we drove between appointments, I silently repeated the acronyms over and over, hoping I would not have to recite them and humiliate myself by mis-sequencing the letters. Teamsters was the only group I didn't feel tongue-tied about. Nevertheless, the actual visits to one office after the next in a two-day period was a seminar packed on labor issues that I took in with great interest.

Being a congressional candidate offered intense learning opportunities. I had to be on the top of multiple issues relevant to Nevadans and the nation. At campaign events and debates where I spoke,

I had to be ready to answer a range of questions. In 2006, my debate preparation consisted of my campaign team running me through a list of topics most likely to come up onstage. Like what I practiced in DC with the Emily's List crowd, I worked on giving politically thoughtful replies that would allow me to walk the fine line between partisan extremes while allowing me to maintain my integrity. When asked something out of my range of experience or expertise, I learned to pivot to a topic with which I was more comfortable.

The key was not to light anyone's hair on fire but to soften any strong opinions on controversial topics as a diplomat might. When my campaign team suggested I equivocate on the capital punishment question, however, I told them, "That's a line in the sand for me. I do not support the death penalty."

Being a perennial student of new topics and ideas was high on the list of priorities I had drafted in a life mission statement I created in some "new age" course I attended back in the day. On the campaign trail, I had to cram learning in because the priority was fundraising, and that kept me on the phone most hours of most days. The good news around fundraising was that I succeeded beyond expectations. The final tally after the end of the campaign was about $1.7 million.

The daily routine of the campaign continued through a busy summer of events around the state. I was on the phone raising money most days, and I attended fundraiser gatherings in the evenings in supporters' homes, often in Reno, where precinct walks in dense neighborhoods were conducted during the days.

The winner of the Republican primary, Dean Heller, in the meantime was working against me. He aired a television ad showing me in an unflattering pose, claiming that as a regent, I had often callously voted to raise tuition on financially struggling students. Steve railed at the TV set when these played; I avoided them. No one likes to see unflattering pictures of themselves blasted out into the airwaves, but I knew it was coming. I thought if that was the Heller team's best shot, they didn't have much ammunition. I recalled an early conversation I had in Washington with DCCC campaign advisors about whether I had any skeletons in my closet that could derail my political campaign. I checked with Steve and reassured the advisors that we had always paid our taxes and there was nothing discoverable in my past that could be damaging.

"Then they will make it up" was their reply, which made me laugh.

The polling consistently showed me trailing Heller in Nevada's hyper-Republican District 2 by only a few percentage points, giving us great momentum. As the November election drew nearer, some polls showed us in a dead heat. As the race tightened, the pressure mounted. In a rally-the-relatives effort, David sent an email to a host of my relatives and close friends from surrounding states, and many showed up to pitch in.

Cousins, friends, and godparents turned out to be a terrific resource and source of moral support. My sister drove down from Oregon to help, along with her daughter, my niece. One second cousin, whose name and paternal connection I knew of but had never met, came up from Napa, California, and stayed through the election to make calls. Another cousin and his wife drove up from Point Reyes, California. They, along with other relatives and friends who had never worked in a political campaign, made calls to strangers who sometimes hung up on them. Weeks before, another cousin living in Utah had come to work a parade in Mesquite, handing out fliers along the route. My daughter's godmother from San Diego flew in to help in those last days, as did another godmother from Sisters, Oregon. I was overwhelmed with everyone's willingness to dive into the hectic and unfamiliar arena of a tight-polling congressional race.

I was deeply touched, reassured, and proud to have this boost of kin support in the closing days of our fourteen-month campaign. Having studied kinship networks in cultures around the world in my graduate student days, I had been struck in the international comparison by how fragmented and expendable American kinship ties were. In the Middle East, the sense of community and obligation within families is tight. Bonds between cousins often mirror those of close siblings. In contrast, in the United States, geographical closeness to family is not a priority in pursuing employment opportunities, and relatives beyond the immediate family rarely gather except for weddings and funerals. A century of mobility has loosened familial roots and kin connection. We have lost something in the shift, and we compensate with friendship networks and work relationships. My awareness of this cultural phenomenon made me all-the-more grateful for my kin who showed up for me to help push my congressional race across the finish line in first place.

The race was close, and the first returns coming in from Reno showed us ahead. Watching those returns come in on the television screens of Atlantis, the Reno hotel where our crush of supporters had gathered, was nerve-rackingly suspenseful. As each update was announced, I held my breath. As returns from outlying counties started to come in and the momentum began shifting, the pressure grew agonizing. About 10:30 in the evening, when most of the Reno precincts had been tallied and returns from the rural counties were dominating the count, David did the math, took me aside, and let me know it was time to concede the race. I made that fateful call I hadn't planned on making and took the stage to let everyone know that we had lost the race. A hushed silence spread as people absorbed the news, although they continued to watch the screen and hope for a miracle.

The worst part about making that concession speech was the feeling I had monumentally let all my supporters down. My family, relatives, and friends, who had come for the last passionate push, had been so supportive, and I felt a sense of desolate failure. Being at the center of the action for a year, I knew how hard everyone had worked for victory. The race had looked to be within grasp of a Democrat for the first time ever. The tight polls had offered hope that we could win; these polls had helped us forget that Nevada's Second Congressional District had always been a Republican district. We had waged one of the strongest campaigns in the state, according to many informed accounts, and we felt our successes could offset the registration disadvantage we faced. But no, despite the impressive size of our win in Reno, with its majority Republican registration, it was the rural counties with their high voter turnout that sealed our fate. When the dust settled and the final analysis was in, we lost by about 5 percent. No Democratic candidate before or since has come so close, but overcoming such a tilted partisan disadvantage was just beyond our reach.

I cannot sugarcoat what it is like to lose a political campaign. It is an emotional gut punch like none other. Fourteen months of a steep learning curve in congressional candidacy, a tireless effort of surmounting new challenges and stressing over critical decisions at every turn, and carrying the responsibility of inspiring others all came down to one cathartic evening in early November. I had put my heart and soul into the effort, and I wanted so much to win. I hoped to bring my voice to the national arena of decision-making and advocate for a more enlightened foreign policy and greater economic fairness on the domestic front. Being the candidate delivers the defeat most personally and is a burden to bear with everyone involved.

"Victory has a thousand fathers, but defeat is an orphan," President Kennedy said.

In my orphaned state, I received hundreds of hugs and consolation messages—they came in person the night we lost, and in the next days and weeks, in phone calls, emails, and letters.

People had their own dashed hopes to deal with, and they were deeply disappointed for the state and for their communities. I knew it was important for me, whom people looked to in leadership, to manage my own grief, be a comfort to others, and model grace and resilience. In my concession speech, I reminded everyone of the fight ahead for the values and principles for which we fought. I urged them to stay in the political arena with the experience they gained for important battles ahead. I thanked them over and over for all they had done and for all we had done together for the noble cause of influencing our democracy. These were the engaged "people" in this government "of the people, by the people, and for the people," without which democracy can't work.

Political campaigns are revved-up environments. Saying farewell to my staff who had moved to Nevada from around the country to work for the campaign was emotionally difficult. We had grown close over those many months of new adventures and hard work, with the same esprit de corps as any athletic team that works with intention and fervor toward the goal of victory. Just as actors come together to produce a Broadway play with a start and finish timeline, a political campaign has an end date, after which team members scatter back to their home bases after emotion-laden goodbyes.

David stayed on for another six weeks for all the wrapping-up activities a large-scale political campaign requires. Having him around was a godsend for me. It gave us time to debrief and process the whole experience since being immersed in it. We particularly shared the reverberation of the loss, which had affected him as much as me.

In David's first go at being a campaign manager and mine at being a candidate in a race of such magnitude, we learned so much about the politics of it all and about each other. We worked closely together, sometimes sleeping in the same room in the limited quarters of volunteers' homes on the many overnight trips the campaign required. I would miss his company, and because it was the final act in the campaign odyssey we had shared, it was the inflection marker signaling it was time to move on. David's career in politics has soared over the years: he headed up the Obama campaign in Nevada and in 2017 founded Forward Majority, an innovative and highly successful national organization that works to affect state legislative races that are now recognized as wielding decisive power in the nation's political balance. David asked me to serve on the Forward Majority board. Our close bond continues to this day.

In the weeks that followed our election loss, as my mind kept pushing me to replay "what if" scenarios that could have produced a different outcome, I found two sources of comfort. In my leadership work with Landmark Education, I had learned about the tyranny of the mind and the eternal struggle required to deny self-defeating thoughts from dominating internal airwaves. This loss was an ultimate test because it had created a wound that my mind pushed me to dwell on. To switch channels and turn down the volume of that inner critic, I reached out to my all-time favorite books to refocus.

Fellow book lovers understand the comfort in returning to a much-loved story for a reread. It is like welcoming an old friend back into your life. For several weeks after the election, my daughter, Tobyn, and I sat side-by-side on the couch and read alternate chapters of Frances Hodgson Burnett's *The Secret Garden* out loud to each other. It is the story of Mary Lennox, a homely, peevish orphan girl from India who is sent to live with her reclusive, sorrowful, widowed, and mostly absent uncle in mysterious Misselthwaite Manor on the Yorkshire moor. When Mary discovers her equally spoiled and peevish invalid cousin, hidden in the hundred-room mansion she is forbidden to explore, together they explore a secret garden locked by tragedy and concealed for a decade. By surreptitiously bringing the neglected plot of forbidden land back to resplendent life, they heal and rekindle themselves and all life in that dark manor on the moor.

Tobyn had been at my side throughout much of the campaign and felt deeply disappointed too. Our book-sharing experience, combined with the loving closeness of family, helped me cross over the summit of sadness and start looking ahead to whatever opportunities might lie beyond this bend in the road. One showed up within six weeks.

It's been generally true in my life that "when one door closes, another opens." Not long after we had closed the books on our 2006 congressional campaign, I got a call from Rebecca Lambe, who headed up Senator Harry Reid's Las Vegas office, asking if we could meet for lunch. She invited Representative Shelley Berkley to join us, knowing of our close friendship. After pleasantries, catching up, and ordering sandwiches, Rebecca asked if I might consider being a candidate to lead the Nevada State Democratic Party as chairperson in the upcoming election.

Once again, I was completely taken aback. I had never been active in Democratic Party organization and had little notion of the role the state party plays. The Douglas County Democratic Party had a yearly barbecue at the Hollister Ranch that I always attended. And over the years, I had occasionally dropped in on the monthly Democratic Central Committee meetings at the Overland Restaurant & Pub in Minden to join a small gathering of the faithful. It was a local joke that Douglas Democrats could hold their meetings in a phone booth, and consequently I had not seen the party's role in elections as definitive. Maybe that was because in Douglas County, they weren't: Republicans filled every elective office in the county. I learned the first time I ran for elective office that party coffers are limited, and when it comes to financing campaigns, candidates are on their own.

Rebecca noted my lack of enthusiasm at the suggestion and began to explain to me the first-time, big-time significance to Nevada in the upcoming election cycle. My ears perked up. I have always chosen to serve in positions that have agency to make a difference, not serve a functionary role. It all came down to the upcoming presidential nomination process, Rebecca explained, the mechanism through which each state votes its preference for presidential candidates and how the tally of all fifty states determines the party's standard bearer. What made the upcoming year, 2008, significant, she said, was the new calendar in this state-by-state process. Nevada's caucus had been moved up to third in the order from a less consequential position. It was a big deal, and thanks to Senator Reid's clout (he was the new majority leader) promoting this change in the national party, Nevada was going to play a central role in the upcoming election cycle.

What is widely known is that the first states hosting primaries or caucuses have outsize influence in which candidate wins the party's nomination. This crucial "early power" explains why presidential candidates have flocked to Iowa and New Hampshire in the years before the active nomination season begins. For Nevada to move up to third on the calendar would mean the state would, for the first time, have a major influence on which candidates advance in the early stages. It would bring all aspiring presidential candidates to Nevada early to actively campaign and would shine the national spotlight on the state in the process—a sought-after prize in the world of presidential politics.

What had stirred the National Democratic Party to reconsider the order of states were the lack of diversity in Iowa and New Hampshire and the concern that their homogenous populations were not representative of the rest of the country. Nevada's inclusion would add to the mix a state in the West with a large Hispanic population. South Carolina, chosen to be fourth, would represent the South with a large African American population. The demographic logic was compelling, and Reid's position as the majority leader gave Nevada a decided advantage in party politics. With the national spotlight trained on Nevada in the 2007–2008 cycle, the priority emerged to have a party leader who was media savvy, capable of effectively hosting presidential candidates, and accustomed to playing a role in the world of national politics. My interest in the position ratcheted up.

This early placement in the presidential nomination process was a huge windfall for Nevada, but it came with a significant challenge—one that I didn't grasp until I had agreed to accept the nomination and been elected as the Democratic Party's state chair in early 2007. The issue was that Nevada is one of a handful of states that used a caucus process rather than a go-to-your-polling-location-and-drop-in-your-ballot procedure. Caucuses require the actual presence of voters at their local precincts, who then divide into candidate preference groups, lobby undecided voters to join them, and con-clude by tallying the number of supporters for each presidential candidate. In previous years in Nevada, these caucuses were lightly attended and held mostly at the county, not the precinct level. Low attendance was typical because Nevada's caucus was in mid-June, and by that time in the cycle the early states had already locked in the nominee, making Nevada's choice irrelevant.

What faced the Nevada Democratic Party in 2007 then was a selection process on a whole new scale, where each county precinct (there are multiple hundreds) would host a caucus instead of each county. Such an increase in scale of magnitude would require iden-tifying hundreds of locations around the state that could handle the expected crowds, training hundreds of local facilitators to manage these gatherings, and reporting the tally to command central at party headquarters the night of the caucus. The organizational chal-lenge of all this was immense, and we had a year to put the pieces in place. With the national spotlight on us, the last thing we wanted was a fiasco.

We hired out-of-state experts with caucus experience for this massive statewide organizing effort. I played a mostly ceremonial role, since what I knew about caucus organization could be writ-ten on the back of a stamp. What did come to pass, and what I did enjoy, was meeting and introducing the candidates on multiple occa-sions. Hillary Clinton, Barack Obama, Joe Biden, Bill Richardson, and others visited Nevada cities multiple times. It was the first year Nevada was seen as important in the presidential election process, and Nevadans across the state flocked to campaign events, enjoying multiple opportunities to meet presidential candidates face-to-face. At the Democratic presidential debate in Las Vegas, as state chair, I welcomed the candidates to the stage and later introduced my adult children to Obama.

My comfort and ease in the role of introducing our nation's political luminaries brought me more opportunities to do so. In 2016, I would introduce Elizabeth Warren, a senator from Massa-chusetts, who was stumping for Clinton, to a crowd in Carson. We both stood on top of a hay bale, in the back of a hay wagon, to get above the crowd.

The day of the January 2008 Nevada caucuses was frantic. We

had set up multiple phone lines to troubleshoot breakdowns from the hundreds of caucusing sites around the state, but issues we had not foreseen arose. We had made a massive effort to let voters know the location of their caucusing sites, but many got lost or went to the wrong site where they were not registered. We had expected a large turnout, but not *so* large! Our trained coordinators were calling us in a panic: Some venues could seat only seventy-five to one hundred people, and two hundred voters had turned up. At another too-small venue, voters were lined up around the block in the rain. We got calls about the caucusing process itself and people complaining and not understanding how they were supposed to proceed. I have no idea how we managed to keep the confusion and disarray in-house, but we did; and in the end, we pulled the caucuses off in the view of the national media that had gathered for the big night. Getting in and tabulating all the tallies from around the state took until midnight, and in a close election, Clinton came in first with Obama a close second.

Complaints flooded in when it was all over. People reported overflowing crowds, inadequate instructions, lack of supplies, and general disorder and discontent. Calls were raised to abandon the caucus practice for the easier and more private primary election process of using polling stations and ballot boxes. Caucuses are public political events. Everyone present can see where you stand, which candidate you are backing. Some voters are uncomfortable with this kind of transparency. Others, however, find support in the sense of solidarity that comes with talking politics in a safe environment and in the old-fashioned nature of advocating for your candidate of choice to others.

I liked the caucus process and saw two overwhelming benefits in it, despite the chaos and inconvenience of having to gather. First, people in individual caucuses got to see who in their neighborhoods and communities were Democrats. This knowing was a powerful connector. In a highly Republican County such as Douglas, I heard many surprised whispers: "I didn't know so-and-so was a Democrat." My own family, who caucused in our Douglas County Foothill site, came away feeling solidarity and connection with several neighbors in what formerly seemed a bleak partisan landscape. In anthropological terms, the gathering at the caucus sites was a gathering of the tribes and reinforced tribal connections. Of course, standing in the center of the caucus-tallying melee in Las Vegas that evening with national media flashing incoming results from multiple monitors, I smiled at the thought: Forty years earlier, a crystal ball would have clouded over at the unlikely prospect of my journey from Goldwater girl to Democratic Party leader. I'd evolved.

A second positive outcome of our statewide caucus efforts was the organization-building aspect and the links that developed between geographically dispersed groups in the nation's seventh largest state by area. Stronger networking capacity was a boon to Nevada's Democratic Party.

There is value in having done something new. After a year as the Democratic Party's state chair, I stepped away. It wasn't a position I would have sought on my own, but it was great to step into that leadership role at the time of Nevada's entrée into the lofty ranks of states that make the biggest difference in the presidential nomination process.

State political parties are strange entities in the conglomerate of political organizations. They are working horses, not show horses. Rarely power brokers in a state's internal political operations, they share data sets and precinct information that are invaluable to political campaigns. They are especially helpful in providing critical boots on the ground and networking. As in so many organizations, their effectiveness can rest with the right leadership and the support they get from their senators and congressional representatives. In the case of Nevada, Senator Reid's close relationship and support for the state party was always foundational in enhancing its effectiveness and impact.

For me, the people are what make any role I have played and any goal I've gone after so rewarding. As the party's state chair, my esteem of Democrats continued to grow—we are a party that celebrates people-centered values, and those who work within the party at state and county levels do it all out of the limelight. My hat is off to the thousands of regular people who give their time, talent, and energies beyond their day jobs to work in the trenches of political activism for better government and the values in which they believe. Democracy cannot work without engaged citizens, and those who work within the party are great patriots who go the extra mile to keep the democratic wheels turning.

In the spring of 2008, I threw my hat in the ring once again to run for the Second Congressional District seat. I had a great campaign team, including the best finance director ever in Chris Anderson, and I figured my name recognition, success in fundraising, and experience as a congressional candidate in the district would give me a leg up despite the large partisan registration disadvantage. This time around, I was running against the incumbent, Dean Heller, who had beaten me in 2006. Incumbency and registration odds confer an advantage I could not overcome. I lost again.

It was time for me to take down my campaign signs and look for new ways to support others and contribute to a progressive agenda wherever doors opened, and opportunities showed up.

CHAPTER 7

National and International Opportunities to Make a Difference

The last elected political position in which I served was as the state chair of Nevada's Democratic Party. I didn't leave politics but took up the baton of an activist citizen through the written word and by attending campaign events and occasional marches. I continue to support good candidates through financial contributions and by hosting fundraisers at our Tahoe home.

Having spent many hours and days on the campaign trail, I relate easily to those who throw their hat in the ring, especially now that the political and civic discourse has become so rancorous and polarized. Ever since President Donald Trump normalized a nasty tenor, many now consider it acceptable. My hat goes off to all those who take the plunge into running for office and giving the public a choice in their government. Democracy won't work without active citizen participation, in whatever form that takes.

Several opportunities to serve my community, my state, and my nation flowed out of the years I spent in elective office. Some of these positions revolved around higher education, and one took me back to the Middle East, a part of the world I like and know well. One had a strictly Nevada focus that inspired my desire to give back to Nevada in a different capacity.

I got a call from Tom Gallagher of Las Vegas in 2008 suggesting we team up to start a think tank. I was intrigued by the idea, aware of the role such organizations play in other parts of the country providing the public with critical information and policy analysis on important topics. Tom had been very supportive of me as a congressional candidate, having run unsuccessfully himself in a Las Vegas congressional district a few years earlier. Tom and I shared a common history in both having worked for Aramco in Saudi Arabia many years earlier. He had been chief executive officer of Park Place

Entertainment most recently, which later became Caesars Entertainment in Las Vegas. After retiring, Tom devoted his life to civic causes, philanthropy, and particularly, education. Tom and I were aligned on many policy issues, and he had become a good friend.

I loved the idea of a think tank but had no idea where to start. I did what everyone does these days: I googled "how to start a think tank." One link heralded a gathering of think tank type institutes and organizations, but when I booked a ticket and visited, I found myself in a conclave of far-right organizations that were all about ideological advocacy and not a gathering where I felt at home or learned much that was to be organizationally valuable.

Tom and I made a list of Nevada leaders who might like to join our effort. He reached out to gaming executive Phil Satre, among others, and I reached out to Joe Crowley and Carol Harter, both of whom had retired from their university presidencies. CPA, entrepreneur, and philanthropist Deane Albright joined us in those small early gatherings at McDonald Carano law offices to brainstorm what it was we wanted to create and how to form this entity to inform and educate policy discussion in Nevada. We decided early on against an advocacy approach but chose instead one which provided balanced, nonpartisan policy research, analysis, and education.

We brought in a couple of consultants from other states with think tank experience to our early meetings around 2011 and added members to bring geographical and political balance. As the organization took shape, it was fittingly Gallagher's idea to name the policy center we were forming after a popular former governor of Nevada, Kenny Guinn, who had died tragically in 2010. Satre stepped into leadership early on, and it was especially his and Tom's support and leadership through the years that allowed the seed of the idea to germinate and become the Kenny Guinn Center for Policy Priorities, a jewel in Nevada's policy landscape, now housed on the UNR campus.

I served as vice chair of the Guinn Center's board for a number of years and then as governance chair. But I stepped aside in 2020 when the leadership demands of the other positions I had assumed required more time and travel than I had available. Because I was at the table in the early days of talk and dreams, it was deeply rewarding to see the Guinn Center grow in stature and statewide reach.

Following my tenure with the Nevada Board of Regents, the Association of Governing Boards of Universities and Colleges (AGB) invited me to serve on the Council of Board Chairs. AGB is the national organization that works to provide boards of regents and trustees with the best advice and support on effective governance and strategic leadership. I had come onto its radar at one of their national conferences in 1998, when I led a group of Nevada regents to showcase the reforms we had enacted on gender equity in the mid-nineties. In my last years as a Nevada regent, AGB invited me to be trained as one of its national consultants to lead board retreats and continuing education sessions for other college and university boards. I have achieved the status of senior fellow with AGB and have loved doing this work that continues to this day.

Nevadans have witnessed considerable strife and contention on the Board of Regents over the years. Having worked with numerous public institution boards over the last decades and bringing a comparative lens to the matter, I can attest that Nevada's public clashes and disputes are not unique to the state. These disruptive conflicts happen in other states as well, although Nevada's board seems to air their unmediated differences in the most public and discrediting ways.

Private university boards select their own members, but public boards must accommodate whoever is elected or appointed. The unpredictability of who serves on the board underscores the importance of system and board leadership to help forge and support a sense of common vision, mission and purpose, and clear role definition and responsibility. Importantly, leadership must have the skill set to work inclusively and build consensus across a diverse set of personalities, politics, and priorities—a daunting leadership challenge in these politically divisive times. Boards appointed by governors and legislatures, as in many states, do not always guarantee more decorum in the board room and can bring in patronage appointments of campaign contributors and political interference in the academic affairs of colleges and universities.

As someone who is passionate about education and who considers it the bedrock of democracy as well as personal, local, and national well-being, I was pleased to keep my hand in, making a useful contribution to the field. I don't have a count of the numerous institutions and states I have visited, offering workshops for college and university leadership reviewing best practices of good governance, assessing board performance, addressing intra-board conflicts, and facilitating conversations around pressing local issues. I have worked internationally as well.

Many cultures of the world honor their elders for the wisdom they have accrued from many decades of living. America isn't one of them. With the youthful fixation that Hollywood spawns, American seniors are too often treated as peripheral, and having little to offer. Experience is the real teacher in life though, and finding more ways to tap into the well of expertise and knowledge of those in post-retirement would serve our country and citizens well. Many retired college and university presidents also serve as AGB consultants, transitioning from administrative leadership to a role of guide on the side, sharing their wisdom in support of good leadership in higher education governance.

Recently, AGB reconstituted its Council of Board Chairs, offering a forum for a national selection of board chairs to meet quarterly. As cochair of this council, I help facilitate spirited peer-to-peer discussions and best-practice sharing around the compelling issues those who govern colleges and universities face today. Many of our nation's colleges and universities are experiencing existential threats related to financial constraints and political interference. Regrettably, as states across the country have pulled back on their commitment to affordable access to postsecondary education through decades of funding cuts, the cost of a college education has been transferred to students and their families. Skyrocketing student loans and student loan debt are the result. There is a price point, however, where students cannot bear the expense, and in some parts of the country, college enrollment numbers are declining. Alternative certification programs in business and industry have drawn students away with a promise of less expense and less lifelong crippling debt. The COVID-19 pandemic has added to the decline in some sectors, particularly among community colleges.

Political interference in the governance of our colleges and universities is a perilous recent development threatening our public institutions. Partisan politics are plaguing this sector and threatening to do irreparable damage. Culture wars, now targeting educational institutions at all levels, are antithetical to the well-being of the American education system, campus culture, and the student learning experience. The form these attacks are taking in colleges and universities focuses on academic freedom, a grounding principle and preeminent value of the American higher education system. The strong academic reputation of American colleges and universities, which draw students from all over the world, is based on an academic philosophy that incorporates curricular diversity and openness to a broad spectrum of ideas, theories, and beliefs—unlike China and other authoritarian countries, which limit courses to those aligned with their ideological doctrines.

Horace Mann, an early American educational reformer who more than any single figure is responsible for the establishment of America's public school system, had strong convictions about the purpose of public education and the importance of keeping sectarian and political influences at bay. Mann advocated for universal public education as a means of building a healthy nation. He proposed that bringing young people of all classes together for a common learning experience would have an equalizing impact on society and would instill common values that could help in character building as well. Although Mann's focus was on K–12 education, the notion of keeping ideological influences away from the educational orbit was central to his philosophy.

Recent efforts of governors and legislatures in several states to undermine the academic freedom that academic tenure ensures and to micromanage curricular content is a serious threat to the integrity of American education philosophy. Efforts to disallow the use of Critical Race Theory (CRT) stand out as the poster child of this regrettable trend. CRT is one theory among many that comprise an education. Efforts to censor the teaching of CRT remind me of pushback against including the works of Karl Marx in my college curriculum.

For students to develop the critical thinking skills that are promised and prized as an outcome of a college education, they must be exposed to a range of ideas and theories. They must be provided with a wide portfolio of knowledge against which to weigh and consider competing ideas and concepts. Teaching that aligns to ideological confines is called indoctrination, not education. It is the fiduciary responsibility of governing boards to protect the independence of our colleges and universities, and of education leaders everywhere to reject the political intrusion that right-wing political actors are trying to impose. Education is the bedrock of democracy, and efforts to protect it from the latest political tide must never waver. I am glad to still be in the game of higher education governance, rallying opposition to these undermining forces.

Another higher education body in which I have been privileged to serve is the National Advisory Committee on Quality and Integrity (NACIQI), which recognizes and evaluates the agencies that accredit our colleges and universities and advises the US secretary of education on higher education policy. Senator Reid appointed me to this national position in 2012. Our job at NACIQI is to hold accreditors' feet to the fire to make sure they are rigorous in their oversight and assessment of the academic quality of programs in our higher education institutions. Accreditation, which colleges and universities must have to be eligible to admit students with federal loans, is the primary quality assurance system on which the American public can rely—it is like the USDA stamp of approval for healthy food products. We at NACIQI are currently refining an academic quality dashboard to assist us in our oversight of these agencies, who are the nation's guarantors of quality to prospective students.

The American University of Iraq, Sulaimani (AUIS), in Iraqi Kurdistan, was established in 2006 near the Iranian border. Iraqi Kurdistan is an independent region in the mountainous north of the country, with its own government, economy, and military—the often written-about Kurdish Peshmerga forces. The US has been close to and protective of this region since the 1990s, when the Kurds were under attack from the Baghdad-based government of Saddam Hussein. Kurdistan is a stable, calm, and economically developed region, distant from the turmoil and violence that often roils regions to the south in Iraq. International news sources don't focus on quiet and peaceful sectors such as the Kurdish region, and my frequent trips there often invite alarmed reactions from those who imagine the entire Middle East as violent and dangerous. Sulaimani is a safe, modern, thriving city, set in a lovely mountainous backdrop. I am occasionally accorded a security escort as the chair of the university's board, but in the Middle East, as elsewhere, security details are as much about status signaling as actual security needs.

Like all American universities abroad, AUIS teaches in English and includes the two-year general education requirement of liberal arts and science courses required for graduation and a baccalaureate degree. American universities abroad are independent stand-alone institutions, connected only loosely through a network to other American universities abroad. In 2012, I was inducted onto the AUIS board because of my governance expertise and connection to the American accreditation process. I have served as vice chair of the board and most recently as chair.

AUIS serves about 1,500 students, 38 percent female, a quarter of whom may wear the traditional hijab (head scarf), but often are on campus in jeans and casual Gen Z attire like students around the world. What particularly fills me with pride is the impact of the liberal arts education we offer. Talking with our fourth-year students and graduates, I am impressed by the way they articulate opinions and think critically about the region's—and world's—challenges. We consider AUIS to be educating the future leaders of the region. Importantly, these American universities abroad are some of the best soft power tools that US foreign policy has. The educational foundation our graduates receive includes a broad portfolio of knowledge and encourages their ability to think through the values of competing ideas. Most universities in the Middle East and in much of the world direct their students straight into occupational tracks according to the specific degree they are pursuing. Engineering students study engineering and medical students, medicine. The uniqueness of the American university abroad model is that it sequences job training in the final years with a liberal arts core in the first years.

In 2019, AUIS partnered with Arbat Brighter Future, a private foundation that offers full-ride scholarships to high school seniors in the nearby United Nations–run Arbat Syrian refugee camp. Artist Florence Robichon and her husband, Rachid, established the scholarship after she spent two years in the camp teaching art while he was heading up a composite company in nearby Sulaimani. At the couple's own expense, Florence showed the refugee children how to decorate their drab cinder block houses with bright murals. She asked them to focus on something they had to leave behind in fleeing the violence in Syria and depict it in art. One little boy drew a picture of his bicycle; another drew his spotted dog.

Before the establishment of the scholarship, kids in the camp, often of well-educated families, had no opportunity to pursue college and careers. Refugees fleeing violence can take almost nothing with them. Providing this path to higher education has enlivened the high school students to study hard to compete for the limited scholarship funds. In 2019, when I visited the camp, along with Steve and Tobyn, we were deeply touched and impressed by the seriousness of the students in their studies, by the bright murals they had created to brighten their drab surroundings, and by their gratitude for being given a new chance in life through education. We are champions of and contributors to the Arbat Brighter Future scholarship program and love being able to help these innocent young people who lost everything because of war and violence.

In 2021, I initiated a project to make a documentary film of the inspiring story of the artist who transformed the Syrian refugee camp with mural art, and the lives of the kids in it, by establishing a college scholarship to the nearby American University. After raising the seed funds for the film, I asked Reno documentarian Gwen Clancy to lead the project. In her characteristic enthusiastic way, she sprung at the opportunity. In the winter of 2021, Gwen and I traveled to northern California to get some early footage of artist Florence in her Palo Alto home and of her touching up a city mural she had painted years earlier.

In June 2022, at the time of our AUIS commencement ceremonies and board meeting, Gwen accompanied me to Sulaimani and spent ten days filming with Florence and Rachid at the refugee camp and on the AUIS campus. She filmed students who had earned scholarships through dedicated study, despite the difficult and crowded conditions of the camp, which experiences intermittent electricity outages and other disruptions. She filmed these scholarship recipients at AUIS as they told their breathtaking accounts of fleeing their homes in the middle of the night amid bombs falling around them. She captured their heartbreaking stories of leaving all their belongings behind, and poignantly, their dreams of a normal future with friends, parties, and college. Hearing these stories gave me a deeply emotional glimpse into the human cost of wars that wrench families from their homes, their friends, their lives, their country of citizenship, and then launch them into void of uncertainty.

I sat in with Gwen at the refugee camp school when she filmed the high school juniors and seniors who are aspiring to win the limited number of scholarships the funds currently provide. What inspired me as much as their drive to succeed in their studies amid bleak and bare living conditions was their vision of graduating from college, getting good jobs, and giving back. They talked of helping their families move out of the harsh conditions of the camp and into good housing in Sulaimani; they talked of finding ways to support other young refugee kids to have opportunities to pursue their dreams. These students recognized what the scholarship could provide for them and did not take education for granted. I was touched by the values they expressed: they didn't aspire to wealth and fancy cars, but to finding ways to assist others similarly victimized by violence and war. Witnessing Gwen film these conversations was sobering and moving. I saw "the better angels of our nature" in this unforgiving environment of a desert refugee camp.

The production crew, Gwen, and I are raising more funds to support full production of the documentary. We're planning shorter clips for social media and promotional events and, hopefully, a thirty-minute film. The film can tell the full story of the Arbat Brighter Future scholarship project, of the artist Florence, the kids, and their colorful murals. The wider the audience we can reach, the more awareness we can raise of this inspiring effort to help the innocent. Children lose their dreams to the wars their governments perpetrate without regard for the human cost, and this film exposes that tragedy alongside triumph and resilience.

In between my early conversations with Gwen about the project and our visit to the refugee camp, I had another opportunity to participate in a historic effort to help innocent student victims of war. In 2021, AUIS rescued more than one hundred Afghan students from the American University of Afghanistan (AUAF) in Kabul. We knew through sources that the American University there was one of the early targets of the Taliban and that most of the students would be in danger. Learning of the fast-approaching Taliban at the gates of Kabul, we reached out to Ian Bickford, president of AUAF, and offered to take up to three hundred of their students if they could be evacuated over to us. We had the dorm space since many of our students had been studying remotely. With his building being fired upon, Bickford was enormously grateful for the rescue offer.

Thus began a tense and frightening scramble with our AUIS president and trustees meeting on Zoom calls with AUAF leaders. In the pandemonium leading up and into those final days before Kabul fell to the Taliban, the US military and State Department had their own priorities, and the Afghanistan students were not among them. We heard through President Bickford that the last students had fled campus just as they finished burning the paper records, and as the Taliban advanced to the campus gates.

The situation in Kabul was desperate. We learned that students who had passports had been directed through text messages and WhatsApp to get to staging areas. They were allowed to carry only a backpack. The first group of twenty-seven students, mostly women, was loaded onto a bus and managed to get through the chaos at the airport on their second attempt. Several of our board members had high-level connections, and working with another group, managed to get a charter plane to those female students, who were sitting on the tarmac at the Kabul airport. After a long delay and several mishaps (one of which being the absence of boarding stairs to the aircraft), these students were flown initially to Doha in Qatar.

One of the many immediate problems we faced was getting visas for these students to enter Sulaimani. Fortunately, we had the help we needed from one of our esteemed board members, currently on a leave of absence, who is the president of Iraq. He obviously had the connections to get that overnight critical task handled.

We had less than forty-eight hours to prepare for this first planeload of rescued students. Anticipating their emotional state and the limited number of personal belongings they would be carrying, we went to the closest mall and purchased twenty-seven pairs of pajamas. Flowers from a florist shop were secured for each dorm room. Bruce Ferguson, AUIS president, Wolfgang Hinck, vice president for academic affairs, and other members of the university's leadership team met the rescued students at about four in the morning at the local airport.

These Afghan students, who had been alarmed when told in Doha that they were headed for Iraq—an "out of the frying pan into the fire" knee-jerk response—were relieved to see the modern Kurdish city of Sulaimani and the beautiful campus of our American University. In the days that followed, our administrative team worked long hours provisioning for the material needs of the students and identifying extra counseling and emotional support resources. These students were considerably traumatized, having left their homes and families behind in their frantic dash to a rescue plane and an uncertain future.

Throughout the crisis, members of our board's executive committee were on daily Zoom calls strategizing about the immediate needs of these distressed Afghan students. We raised funds to provide them with a monthly stipend going forward. We added more counselors to our roster as well as staff to help figure out their academic integration into our university curriculum. When the harried call came from the AUAF president accepting our offer to take students, we had unblinkingly said, "Just get them here, and we'll figure it out!"

The situation was all-consuming for our trustees and administrative team in Sulaimani. There was no time to figure out detailed logistics, but dedicating oneself to raising the funds to support the rescue effort was a priority. We dropped everything, tapped into our networks, and reached out to potential corporate donors. Our president was effusive in his praise for the way our board rose to this unprecedented occasion. I was equally proud to chair a board of trustees with such a big heart and determined spirit.

The second group of students targeted by AUAF for rescue had been loaded onto two buses hours after the first bus got through. This group was not as lucky and was forced to turn back by the crush of desperate mobs at the airport and chaos at the terminal. We tried to track their progress through limited communication sources, through the fog of confusion and panic. Once Kabul fell to the Taliban, this other cohort of students hoping for rescue and staged for evacuation had to wait back in their homes in tense circumstances. We were fortunate to have board members with high-level connections to the Qataris, who alone had communication links to the Taliban. We turned to this network in hope of rescuing more of the students frantic to get out of harm's way. Finally, eighty-two more students were furtively slipped through to the airport to a prearranged chartered flight. They made their way via Doha and to our campus. Most of this group were male.

Over the weeks that followed, our administrative staff and faculty continued in their generous effort to welcome these students with their different culture and language, and to integrate them into classes and the campus community. Fortunately, their instruction in Kabul had been in English, the language spoken on our campus. AUAF sent in its academic vice president (from wherever she had fled) and eventually other staff to help these students begin the process of applying to US and European universities for a more permanent arrangement. We considered them on a year's study abroad program at AUIS, not permanently with us, because the funding we raised could not sustain a longer period. Returning to Afghanistan is not an option in their foreseeable future, so it is in these students' best interest to apply for full-ride scholarships at American or European universities with the potential of work and settlement after obtaining their degrees. The female students we rescued are the lucky ones. Since their desperate flight from Afghanistan, the Taliban has closed off university access and almost all educational opportunities for girls and woman across the country.

As a happy, emotional conclusion to our dramatic rescue of the Afghan students, at our June 2022 commencement in Sulaimani, thirty-three of the students who had fled the Taliban just before their senior year walked across our AUIS stage and were awarded their baccalaureate degrees. President Bickford flew in for the occasion, and the entire crowd erupted in a standing ovation and cheers to celebrate the achievement of those students, which might not have happened without the heroic efforts of many to manage their harrowing escape from the Taliban. I was inspired to be there in that celebratory moment, but the uncertain fate of all those students left behind—particularly the women—weighed heavily on my heart. It has not gone well for them.

Serving in a region of the world that especially needs well-rounded and enlightened leaders, in a university that is producing them, is deeply gratifying. My interaction with our students on numerous occasions has reaffirmed our success in this commitment. Visiting with a small group of recent graduates in a post-board meeting outing in Sulaimani, I received a call from our university president that the Iraqi minister of education was visiting and a dinner with him was taking place in one hour at the Grand Millennium Hotel. As board chair, it was important that I attend.

Not wanting to disappoint the students to whom I had committed for the evening, I asked if I could bring them along.

"Why not?" he said.

The students were a bit wowed by the idea of dining at the fanciest restaurant in the city with the nation's minister of education, who I knew would be accompanied by an entourage of bodyguards. Three extra places were set for them in the circulating dining room atop the Grand Millennium. If I worried that these recent graduates would be shy in the presence of the minister, I needn't have. When the topic of employment opportunities for recent graduates and general economic challenges of the region came up in conversation, I sat back and beamed as our young guests shared their views and offered a few good ideas to spur progress. It wasn't only their comfort in expressing themselves that lit me up, but the values they referenced made me proud. In that moment, I knew we were doing a fine job at our American University in Iraqi Kurdistan. To listen to the minister gush over how very impressed he was with our graduates after the meal was icing on the cake. Our president, Bruce Ferguson, beamed with pride as well.

During the last ten years as my engagement in higher education has focused nationally and internationally, I have kept my eye on Nevada's colleges and universities. It has been rewarding to see them continue to grow in size and stature but dismaying to follow the periodic turmoil surrounding the Board of Regents.

For decades there have been efforts by ballot initiative to challenge the constitutionally derived authority of the board and change the means of selecting regents from election to appointment by the governor and legislature. As someone who has worked nationally with numerous appointed boards across the country, I know that the change from election to appointment is not the guaranteed panacea some predict it will be to a highly functioning board. Placing the responsibility of selection of regents into the hands of elected officials can introduce political patronage and ideological bias into the equation in ways that could undermine the academic independence of Nevada's colleges and universities. Too often those elected to office prefer to appoint those who share their political affiliation and to reward their biggest campaign contributors with prestigious appointments. In any system of appointment, those impulses must be guarded against.

Despite the occasionally fraught disposition of Nevada's elected Board of Regents, the long trajectory of our colleges and universities under their governance is impressive. Nevadans have an array of excellent in-state options in postsecondary education that they didn't have forty years ago, and their role in educating citizens whose expertise is advancing Nevada economically is commendable. No enterprise glides effortlessly to greatness, and for all its lack of adequate funding and occasional wobbles our higher education institutions in Nevada do its citizens proud.

My mother and her mother were schoolteachers, so no wonder the field of education drew me to its ranks. In a home full of books, a love of learning got instilled early in my life, and I consider it a core component of a life worth living. Books open endless worlds that are only within reach through their pages. My grandmother had a bookplate which spoke for me, "There is no frigate like a book to take us lands away."

The gift of education is one that enriches lives in myriad ways. What higher calling could there be?

There is great satisfaction in being able to continue contributing to an enterprise that is so vital in so many profound ways. Even more than the personal advantage an education confers is its value to a civil society. A democracy cannot work without an educated citizenry to protect against the vulnerability to propaganda and the tyranny of a would-be autocrat. I am privileged to continue working to help protect the system of higher education and its governance structures and its integrity from the range of threats a polarized citizenry poses.

Those committed to the viability of the American experiment are facing an "all hands on deck" moment. Just a decade ago, few people could have imagined that our democracy was vulnerable to internal subversion, or that a significant percentage of citizens would look favorably on a shift to authoritarian rule. But, considering the January 6 uprising, Americans have learned that we are not immune to those who foment fears of distrust in our electoral process.

A dangerous game, one that is toxic to democracy, is being played. The future will be decided by those of us who take up the gauntlet of active citizenship to protect a government "of the people, by the people, and for the people."

At the end of the day, my journey all started in a serendipitous moment when I said "yes" to an unreasonable offer and jumped off a ledge into the unknown waters of campaign politics. My story is a testament to one strategy for navigating a life that stays open to possibilities and to detours off a charted course. Doing the unexpected opened me to an unpredictable future that unfolded in amazingly gratifying ways. Who could have known?

An early consequence of my rash dive into politics was becoming known in my community as someone with purpose, someone willing to be judged in the public spotlight. After my narrow election loss in 1978, Governor Mike O'Callaghan appointed me to the Judicial Selection Commission, marking the first of many opportunities to follow. Had I not expressed my willingness to step out of the shadows of political grousing and put some skin in the game, that first appointment might never have come. Talk about a fork in the road.

Engaging in one's community and in worlds beyond one's borders is part of the secret of unlocking unforeseeable opportunities. Playing small and safe is an option in life, but taking that approach is nowhere near as exciting as taking a chance with a new direction and discovering ways synchronicity can show up to point the way. I recommend running for something, seeking an appointment, or starting a campaign. Never has the country needed more of its best citizens to step up to the plate.

If national or state level office is not your cup of tea, opting for an appointment to a board or commission allows you to make your voice heard in critical civic settings. School and library boards need the brightest among us to offset the partisan radicals ready to squeeze the curriculum of classes into a rigid ideological lane and by banning books and outlawing topics that reflect the racial and gender diversity of our times. In the spirit of Horace Mann, let's continue to ensure that our public education system reinforces the values of a free society and brings unity instead of division to our fractured nation.

In the end, I owe a lot to Nevada, the land of my birth. It is easy to get lost in the crowds of New York or California, but Nevada, with its smaller population, allowed me the opportunity to step up, stand out, and be heard. In our cherished land of sage and pine, there is space to speak up and make a difference for a future that serves us all. Saying "yes" to challenges near and far has worked for me; it can work for you.

About the Author

JILL DERBY earned a BS from the University of California, San Francisco, her BA from the University of Las Vegas, Nevada, and both her MA and PhD from the University of California, Davis. Her political activism started in the seventies with her involvement in Nevada's effort to ratify the Equal Rights Amendment. In 1988, she was elected to the first of three six-year terms on the Nevada Board of Regents. She was the Democratic candidate for Congress in Nevada's Second Congressional District in both 2006 and 2008.

Derby is currently a senior fellow and senior consultant with the Association of Governing Boards of Colleges and Universities. She is also the chair of the Board of Trustees of the American University of Iraq, Sulaymaniyah, Kurdistan. She stepped down in 2022 from her ten-year service on the National Advisory Committee on Institutional Quality and Integrity, an appointment made by Senator Harry Reid in 2012.